Missouri Armories

Missouri ARMORIES

THE GUARD'S HOME IN ARCHITECTURE AND HISTORY

ROBERT P. WIEGERS

To Joe
a little light reading
for you in retirement
Robert Wiegers

Truman State University Press
Kirksville, Missouri

Cover images: St. Louis Light Artillery Armory Association Armory, see fig. 3.2; Bequet-Ribault House, Ste. Genevieve, see fig. 2.1; 1138th Military Police Company Armory, see fig. 4.19; 1137th Military Police Company Armory, see fig. 5.31; Howard M. Garrett Memorial Armory, see fig. 6.7; Company C, 135th Signal Battalion Armory, see fig. 7.16.

Cover design: Teresa Wheeler

Library of Congress Cataloging-in-Publication Data

Wiegers, Robert P., 1947–
Missouri armories : the Guard's home in architecture and history / Robert P. Wiegers.
        pages cm
Includes index.
ISBN 978-1-61248-063-3 (pbk. : alk. paper) — ISBN 978-1-61248-064-0 (ebook)
1. Armories—Missouri. 2. Military architecture—Missouri. 3. Missouri. National Guard—Facilities. I. Title.
NA4482.M8W54 2012
725'.1809778—dc23

                                                                                                2012002482

To Carrington Barth Wiegers, Specialist
B Company, 7th Battalion, 159th Combat Aviation Brigade
101st Airborne Division (Air Assault)
Ft. Campbell, Kentucky
And to
Trevor Clark Wiegers, 1st Lieutenant
C Troop, 5th Squadron, 73rd Cavalry Regiment (ABN) (RECON)
82nd Airborne Division
Ft. Bragg, North Carolina

Contents

Illustrations, Map, and Table

Acknowledgments

This study benefited from a decade of Central Methodist University student participation. A few of those student historians are Alison Dice, Mark Fowler, Susan Hart, Linda Heringer, Matt Milner, Lucinda Reynolds, Latham Scott, Allyne Solomon, Christina Thompson, Scott White, and Travis Young. Two research grants assisted in the collection of information: a grant from the Missouri Department of Natural Resources, Grant Project Number 29-96-11100-425, November 1997, and a second grant from the Missouri National Guard, Environmental Management Office, Contract R838970053, August 1999.

The Central Methodist University Smiley Library, the Missouri State Archives, the Missouri Historical Society (St. Louis), and the State Historical Society of Missouri (Columbia) assisted the project. Special thanks to Tiffany Patterson, Missouri Historic Preservation Office, for architectural advice. Charles Machon, Regina Meyer, John Viessman, and Orval Henderson were founts of information about the Missouri Guard. Thanks to Bill Barnes, Susan Beattie, David Denman, Bob Harms, Steve Mitchell, and Steven Quackenbush for reading and suggestions. Thanks to Chuck MacFall for photographic work and travel to distant points in the state. Finally, special thanks to those who answered questions over a long gestation period, Maryann Rustemeyer, John Finley, Joy Flanders, and especially to my loving spouse, Martha, and my sons for allowing me to indulge my curiosity.

Foreword

Missouri's militia, today known as the Missouri National Guard, enjoys a history of more than two hundred years of public service. First organized at Ste. Genevieve in 1751, the militia's history is recorded by specific time periods. A select few publications on the Guard are available to readers. In 1934 the Military Council of the Missouri National Guard published a *History of the Missouri National Guard* that primarily details unit activities during World War I and selected postwar events. A second, and more important history is Dr. John Glendower Westover's *Evolution of the Missouri Militia into the National Guard of Missouri 1804–1919*. Written as a dissertation in 1948, this work was published in 2005 by the Missouri Society for Military History. Both books are limited in overall scope. There are a few unit histories: the 138th and 140th Infantry Regiments and 129th Field Artillery Regiment from World War I, a brief 1939 "college yearbook" style history of the Guard and Naval Militia, and a history of the post–World War II Missouri Air National Guard. Other than newspaper stories and scattered articles in periodicals, pertaining to specific events, readers are left with many unanswered questions.

Now comes Dr. Robert Wiegers with his new book on the Missouri National Guard, explaining the Guard's connection with individual communities, through the architecture and public use of many armories. The extraordinary number of photographs connect his descriptive text to the many structures with which all readers, especially guardsmen, are familiar. Dr. Wiegers's book connects nineteenth-century armories to the present.

The Missouri National Guard, including all commanders and adjutants general, should welcome this new book. The book has a place in all armories with a copy at each unit and in the personal library of every reader who enjoys Missouri history—particularly past and current guardsmen.

Lt. Col. (Ret.) Orval L. Henderson Jr.
St. Louis, Missouri
October 21, 2011

Foreword

This volume was a labor of love for Dr. Robert Wiegers, a retired Missouri National Guardsman and the proud father of two sons, Carey and Trevor, who now serve with the 101st Airborne and 82nd Airborne Divisions, respectively. Dr. Wiegers traces the origins—and in some cases fates—of armories throughout the state, examining the armories and how they reflect the Missouri National Guard's character, history, and place in the community.

The story of our armories isn't a story about buildings. It's the story of generations of citizen-soldiers and airmen, and the families and communities that supported them. It is the story of how the United States shifted from a colonial wilderness into one of the most technologically and economically advanced nations in the world. It is the story of how art, architecture, and culture influenced the most utilitarian of structures. It is the story of how major international events affected small towns across the state.

Dr. Wiegers writes, "The ideal armory is a place where guardsmen feel pride in membership. It should also be a building the community can take pride in as well." Those words are true about today's armories more than ever. Armories are where our new enlistees go through the Recruit Sustainment Program to prepare them for the rigors of basic training. Armories are where our current soldiers and airmen spend their monthly drills and, often, their annual training. Armories are where our retirees return to mentor the generations that carry on their service and traditions.

In a study of dozens of buildings built over hundreds of years, Dr. Wiegers examines what makes some armories beloved landmarks while others are ultimately demolished or forgotten. He examines the diverse influences that shaped our armories, from the Spanish, French, English, and colonial traditions, all the way through the Cold War and into the modern era. He shows the changing role of the armory from a necessary form of protection in colonial times to a community center and sign of prosperity in modern times. Yet through it all, there is one common feature: the citizen-soldier.

You'll find some familiar faces in these pages. Capt. Harry S. Truman and Capt. Charles Lindbergh, two of the Missouri National Guard's iconic figures, are both featured. But given equal time are men and women who are usually known only in the communities where they served. There was Capt. Frank M. Rumbold, a soldier and renaissance man who found a home for Battery A in St. Louis at the turn of the century. There was Capt. C. E. Fowler, who worked to draw attention to the deteriorating conditions in which his soldiers were working in Kennett in the 1930s. There was Col. James E. Rieger, a World War I hero to whom the Kirksville Armory is dedicated. These pages include dozens more citizen-soldiers whose contributions, great and small, have made the Missouri National Guard the proud institution it is today.

I hope you enjoy this volume as much as I did. It is a fitting tribute to the men and women who have served in communities throughout Missouri and on countless battlefields throughout the world.

Maj. Gen. Stephen L. Danner
Adjutant General, Missouri National Guard

Introduction
Historians and Heralds

Likening the National Guard to a profit-oriented national corporation may seem like comparing apples to oranges, but in many respects the Guard is a national corporation with local franchises. A national corporation has a corporate headquarters, the Guard has the state adjutants general's office. A corporation has local offices, each with its own workforce, the Guard has companies and brigades. And in place of a branch office or store, the National Guard has the armory. The raison d'être for a national corporation is to make money by providing a service or selling a product, whereas the National Guard's mission is to render a public service as a general emergency response and reserve military force.

Like a corporation selling its services or products, the Guard shares major challenges in marketing and brand identification. The corporation uses public relations specialists to craft a positive public image and to attract new customers. In the Guard, historians and heralds act as public relations specialists; the historian chronicles the lifestyle and accomplishments of the group, while the herald presents the group's history and successes to the public. Both the historian and the herald play important roles in promoting the Guard and influencing public opinion.

The National Guard has a particular need for dedicated penmen like the historian and the herald. Without public relations specialists, corporations risk losing brand loyalty and market share; the National Guard risks losing its local identity and appeal to the volunteer-spirited. As a service organization that draws its manpower from across the state, the National Guard needs a good corporate image to fill the ranks and maintain political support.

Like the corporation that courts the consumer to buy its product, so the National Guard courts the recruit. Comparing recruits to consumers is instructive since it touches on the reasons why some potential recruits decide to join the Guard and others do not. If a potential consumer is given a choice between a known brand-name product and an unknown one, the consumer will most likely pick the option with the best reputation or look elsewhere. The same applies to the National Guard recruit-consumer when given a choice between joining service groups such as the Boy Scouts, Rotary, American Legion, Army Reserve, or the Guard—the best reputation will win.

Because the consumer can be swayed by an attractive image as well as price, national corporations are careful to promote their corporate identities in a way that will guide the consumer to choose their product. This idea has led to the proliferation of registered symbols, colors, and building styles, such as McDonald's golden arches, the Greyhound Bus's racing greyhound, John Deere's signature shade of green, Walmart and Home Depot's distinctive building designs, and Gateway's black and white cow-patterned boxes. Since the armory is the Guard's version of the local office or franchise storefront, the visual appeal of its architecture is just as important as the golden arches are to McDonald's corporate image.

The process that creates a winning corporate image for the Guard begins with the historian. The challenge for the historian is to document Guard activities that bolster a popular mystique. Although the Army National Guard is the oldest reserve to the regular army and shares a rich history with it, the Guard itself also has a long and equally rich story. Missouri provides the historian with a whole range of military lore to make this state a centerpiece of militia and National Guard historical studies. Located in the middle of the country but having a colonial heritage, and having joined the Union in the early nineteenth century before armories developed a distinct architectural style, Missouri has all the traditions of the earliest militia and also inherited eastern architectural traditions that frame the only true National Guard home—the armory building. In contrast, most western states initiated an American-style militia after the armory was an accepted militia feature.

In Missouri, the historian can begin with the early French tradition of *place d'armes* musters and trace all national refinements in militia and developments in National Guard architectural styles since colonial times. The only armory styles not found in Missouri are regional variations common to the east and southwest. Without a Dutch or English colonial presence in Missouri, few examples of armories with Dutch colonial or Georgian features are found in the state, and without significant Spanish influence, few armories are found with Spanish colonial elements. Despite the early history of French colonization along the Mississippi River in Missouri, French architectural styles did not influence later armory development, perhaps because by the time armories were being built, so many other ethnic groups had settled in the area that French building traditions were diluted. Another significant difference in Missouri armories is the reason for building the armory in a certain place. Some eastern armories were built as instruments of social control—to intimidate the working class. In contrast, selecting a location for an armory in Missouri was often based on a desire for community improvement and social cohesion, similar to how construction of religious structures and cultural buildings reflects on local society and supports the community. Regardless of how the armory looks or how the Guard acquired the building, the local armory served both the Guard and the community. Since the armory is the only physical proof of the Guard's presence in most municipalities, it is the local face of the Guard—its corporate image.

Foremost among the motivations for this research is to record one aspect of the Missouri Army National Guard's corporate heritage. Instead of tracing the activities and operations of a Guard unit, this study concentrates on the armory as the most visible aspect of Guard history and uses it as a focal point to highlight other facts. Although this work is intended as a reference and an exploration of Missouri armory development, the collected information is not exhaustive, for many armories and the many units that served in them are unknown—proof that the Guard historian's job is never finished. Because so many armories have disappeared, and along with them, the units that called them home, every armory should be considered a heritage asset for the Missouri National Guard. Unfortunately, because of armory distribution and the diverse forms of their architecture, many armories have blended in with the surrounding landscape too well and for so long that they have already been forgotten.

A typical small-town forgotten armory is the "old armory" in Fayette, Missouri (see fig. 2.47). The 1905 building is a tall, three-story brick structure on the southeastern corner of the Fayette courthouse square, affectionately known as the "old opera house." It is still easy to imagine where storefronts once occupied the three ground-level bays with two stories above. This grand old building dominates the corner where it housed the town opera house, then the local National Guard armory, a garment factory, and finally a church.

To fully grasp the position of the armory in Guard history, it is necessary to document the gradual emergence of this new building type and follow its refinement from the time the Guard met informally in public places, such as alehouses, to modern times when the local armory serves not only as the Guard's home, but also as a civilian emergency shelter. This study includes architectural and historical notes, providing a context that expands the understanding of armory development in conjunction with the evolution of the National Guard. All armories in this study are divided into categories based on architectural styles, with each category being roughly equivalent to a specific historical time period. The use of categories allows easy comparison of buildings within and between groups. These categories also allow Missouri armories to be compared with armories in other states and allow architectural historians in other states to use these same categories, tailoring them to their own circumstances and adding regional styles that predate or postdate those found in Missouri.

Unlike monuments, former armories are typically undocumented and unseen, in part because former Guard historians and heralds failed to recognize this important part of Guard history, and planners failed to appreciate the importance of corporate architecture to the Guard image. But the National Guard armory can be a vital link between past and present and a durable tie between the Missouri Guard and the community. Former armories symbolize the longevity and the dedication of all guardsmen; the only other structure that provides any type of memorial to the Missouri National Guard is the Museum of Missouri Military History at the Ike Skelton Training Site near Jefferson City, established in 1999.

The museum contains valuable information on the history of the Missouri National Guard, but the armories scattered throughout the state demonstrate, on a daily basis, the close relationship between the Guard and the community. Guardsmen may see the armory as the home of the Guard and probably see armories in their area, whether decommissioned or still in use, as providing a sense of belonging and attachment. Civilians may see the armory as a community center or landmark, and may derive a sense of security from having a Guard armory in the community. In the nearly four centuries since the first militia, armory designs have been affected by evolving architectural styles, technological developments, changes in space needs and use, and the needs of the community. However armory styles develop and evolve, this most visible and enduring symbol of the National Guard will continue to provide guardsmen and community members with a tangible connection to the National Guard.

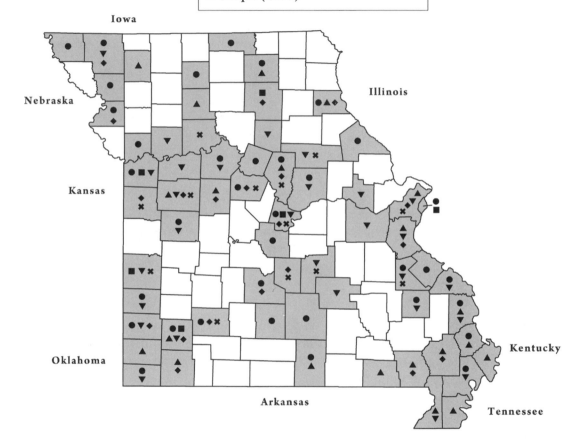

Chapter 1
Discovering the Armory

"So instead of calling it an armory, I prefer to call it the home of the guardsman."
Brigadier General R. E. Rilea, Oregon National Guard

W hen we think of military architecture, we usually think of fortresses and castles or something equally massive and intimidating. The armory, however, falls into a different category of military architecture because it serves a different function. In 1935 congressional hearings on funding for National Guard armories, Brigadier General R. E. Rilea, vice president of the National Guard Association, correctly described the armory as "the home of the guardsmen, the storage place for the Federal property . . . the community center . . . [and] a haven in time of catastrophe." Because the armory fills multiple functions, serving both a part-time military force and the broader community, armory design has acquired a community rather than a martial image. Although some armory buildings may resemble a fortress in size and embellishments, the greater number are domestic with sparse martial symbolism, intended to welcome the visitor rather than repel the invader.

The function and design of the modern National Guard armory is not an accident of history or architectural whim. The armory's function clearly evolved over time, as each generation of Americans tinkered with an inherited militia organization based on the citizen-soldier model, which is based on the idea that the citizen has an obligation to arm himself to defend his country. This is in contrast to the practice of hiring mercenaries or having a professional standing army. The very idea of an armory located within a civilian environment has roots in the colonial history of the American military system, which has both a federal standing army and part-time state militias. The American militia system is a variant of the European approach to war with accepted norms and conventions that dictate how war is prepared for, conducted, and memorialized.[1] In the years leading up to the American Revolution, many colonists objected to the practice of having a standing army that might act independently of civil authorities, believing that a citizen-soldier would protect the freedom of the people because he is a civilian. The colonial militia was formed around the idea of the citizen-soldier, and in the early years of the new republic, state and federal authorities debated the merits of having a militia of citizen-soldiers under the command of the state versus having a standing army under the command of the central government. Under the militia system, each citizen-soldier was responsible for supplying his own gun and equipment, and met to drill at regular intervals. This meant that the militia unit needed a place to meet, but needed little else. Since cultures change over

1. Keegan, *A History of Warfare*, xi. See also Hanson, *Carnage and Culture*.

1

time, the shape and function of war-related buildings have also changed. As the American military system shifted to one that relied on a central standing army with local militias acting to supplement the standing army in times of emergency, it became clear that the armories needed to change to meet a new set of needs. Major factors at the national level that have governed changes in military building design include the availability of federal funds for armory construction, political priorities, and international relations that affect the need for military preparedness and the size of the armed forces. To a lesser degree, these factors function on the state level and have influenced armory considerations since colonial times.

For many years, existing community buildings could serve the needs of the local National Guard unit. In Fayette, for example, the building that served as the armory from 1922 to 1941 was at various times the town opera house, a garment factory, and a church. On the ground level, stores once occupied the three bays. Today the building houses a sports bar and is barely distinguishable from the other buildings around it. The earliest armories would have provided, at a minimum, space for a drill hall and room for storage. Today an armory needs a large space for a drill hall, room for storage, an arms vault, and office space for unit administration. Modern armories often also have a kitchen, a firing range, a recreation area, and other amenities that vary from place to place, but are not essential. While the basic requirements of the armory building may be fairly uniform, the building design or style itself does not have to conform to any special requirements, making it possible for an armory to be housed in almost any type of building.

Some armories have survived for generations in the American cityscape and have become symbols of architectural development as well as National Guard history. It is impossible to estimate how many Americans served in all state Guard establishments, but it is possible to estimate the number of buildings guardsmen have utilized as armories nationwide. Extrapolating from the 220 documented armories in Missouri yields an approximation of ten thousand armories throughout the country. Clearly, every town did not have an armory, but it is likely that most large- to medium-size cities, and many small towns, such as Burlington Junction, Missouri (population 813 in 1935), had an armory at one time or another. Currently the Army National Guard has a presence in over three thousand American communities.

Since the early 1800s, the presence of a National Guard armory has always been a good talisman for city prosperity and a sign of civic pride. In 1907, the editor of the *Perryville Sun Newspaper* put it plainly:

> Now, we don't want the outside world to understand that there was any need for the establishment of a Guard here to maintain the peace or order of this city, but we might as well have one here, as they have one in nearly every town of any great importance in the state, and it don't [*sic*] cost a person anything to belong to it; the government pays all expenses. No, Perryville is a peaceable town, don't you forget that, but it is deserving of everything that any other city in the State is, and hence the organization of the National Guard here.[2]

Everyone in a small-town economy benefited from the presence of a Guard unit. In addition to the small stipend the state allotted for armory rent—in 1900 about twenty-five dollars per month— the payroll was considerable and regular. At one time, in communities smaller than regional cities or county seats, the Guard armory and the post office may have been the only outside sources of

---

2. "National Guard Organized," *Perry County* (MO) *Sun,* June 6, 1907.

income injected into an otherwise agrarian economy. If the armory was rented, it might have been in a ground-level storefront or on the second floor. If the building was built privately by the unit through membership pledges, or built by the state with matching federal funds in the 1930s, the community had a state-of-the-art armory. From here the local Guard unit conducted its business in full view of the community.

Historians who want to interpret the National Guard must understand the role of the armory to the unit and the community. The armory is the center around which everything in the unit marches. All official Guard training at one time began at the armory. Wintertime training at the unit level lays the groundwork for instruction at the regimental and division levels conducted each summer.[3] In addition to its military functions, the armory is open to community use and in many towns and cities that host a Guard unit, the armory is the most frequently used location for civic and social events. The armory also plays a role in recruiting for the National Guard. The adjutant general's *Biennial Report* for 1907–1908 noted the varying quality of armories across the state and the relationship between the condition, and identified good armories as a major influence in successful recruiting:

> The buildings used as armories by the companies stationed at the various towns and cities over the State vary greatly in suitability for the purpose. At some points the efforts and means of the members of the company have provided fairly adequate quarters; at others they are very poor. Proper quarters can be secured in every instance if fair rental can be paid. With the small appropriation available this has not been possible. In every case where a suitable armory has been provided, an excellent company will be found. If the Guard is to attain the highest degree of efficiency sufficient funds must be appropriated to pay fair rentals and provide proper maintenance.[4]

In 1912, the War Department reported fourteen out of sixty-three unit armories in Missouri were so shabby as to discourage enlistments or reenlistments.[5] The message from 1912 is still applicable today; the corporate architecture of the armory is important. But as important as the armory is to the life of the National Guard, the history of the armory is neither simple to understand nor easy to discover, as the history of the home of the Guard is closely intertwined with the history of the organization.

The Militia Setting

The best way to understand the rise of the armory is to trace it alongside the development of the National Guard. The two trajectories do not exactly match, yet changes in the armory do follow advances in Guard history. The Missouri National Guard began as a French militia, then became a Spanish militia, and finally an English-American-style militia, as the territory changed hands and successive governments tried to control events and populations while investing little in defense. The development of the Missouri Guard was therefore influenced by a complex mixture of social, political, and economic factors. To offset the expense of supporting a regular army, all colonial powers in North America utilized the concept of the citizen-soldier to some degree. An organized, armed body of citizens was identified as an ordinary or common militia in which all males between certain

---

3. Division of Militia Affairs, *Report, . . . 1911*, 18.

4. Adjutant General, *Report . . . 1907–1908*, 27.

5. Division of Militia Affairs, *Report, . . . 1912*, 45.

ages were required to supply their own arms and participate in several daylong musters a year. During a muster, the citizen-soldier learned to use a gun and master the battlefield drill of the time. This service was a duty owed by all colonists. On the East Coast, this obligation derived from Anglo-Saxon traditions that came with the English colonies in America.[6]

European-style militias operated within the boundaries of the future state of Missouri as early as the eighteenth century. A few cultural practices differentiated the French and Spanish from the English militias, such as their reliance on a standing army, restriction on the ownership of weapons, and their willingness to recruit nonwhites into militia service. The French had scant regular army forces outside of eastern Canada and New Orleans to garrison the Upper Mississippi Valley. Colonial governors relied on the militia as a replacement body for the regular army in their western settlements.[7] Every male between fifteen and sixty years was attached to a local militia company and expected to drill regularly. Militiamen were responsible for supplying their own weapons and did not have standardized uniforms. When the need arose, the French colonial authorities ordered levies from the militia to fill the ranks of regular army units.

The earliest record of a militia in Missouri comes from Ste. Genevieve in southeast Missouri. In 1751, the commandant of the Illinois Country, Jean Jacques Macarty, commissioned a census that included the Parish of Sainte Anne, composed of its major towns on the Illinois side of the river and the west bank community of Ste. Genevieve, the first permanent colonial settlement on the Missouri side of the great river.[8] The name Andre Deguire *dit* Larose (i.e., "called Larose") appears on the census as captain of the Ste. Genevieve militia, making him the first recorded militia member in the future state of Missouri.[9] Deguire was a wealthy citizen with a large family and substantial land holdings. As militia captain, he also filled many other roles in the colonial French social order not directly associated with militia.[10]

French militia companies mustered for training on the village square or common field, a location suited for infantry drills involving large bodies of men. Since each militiaman supplied his own weapons and clothing, there was little need for storage space. Powder and ball for a regional emergency was cached in a government building or the local militia captain's house. In the case of Andre Deguire in Ste. Genevieve, he was noted in the 1751 census as the owner of the only gunpowder and shot in town. The Chouteau House in St. Louis was probably used for storage also. Often referred to as Government House, it was a stone building, centrally located, and the home of the militia captain.[11]

French administration of the Louisiana Territory was conveyed to Spain under the 1762 Treaty of Fontainebleau. Spanish dignitaries arrived in the area of Missouri in 1770. They added depth to the defense structure with a larger contingent of the Spanish regular army than had been present during the French administration.[12] Under Governor Alejandro O'Reilly, an Irishman in Spanish service, colonial defense was realigned to move a greater share of the responsibility for defense onto the militia. On February 12, 1770, O'Reilly directed the creation of thirteen militia companies in Missouri.[13]

6. Ansell, "Legal and Historical Aspects of the Militia."

7. Billon, *Annals of St. Louis in Its Early Days*, 66–72.

8. See Nelson, "Sainte Anne."

9. Ekberg, *Francois Vallé and His World*, 96.

10. Ekberg, *Colonial Ste. Genevieve*, 29.

11. Billon, *Annals of St. Louis in Its Early Days*, 150, 245.

12. Ekberg, *Colonial Ste. Genevieve*, 56.

13. Holmes, *Honor and Fidelity*, 19.

According to instructions from the Spanish commandant of Upper Louisiana at St. Louis, Charles Delassus, these thirteen companies would muster every fifteen days on Sunday and "each commandant [would] exercise his [men] in marching by file, or in sections of four and eight, according to the number of their men, to teach them the manual of loading and firing, to enable them to execute it promptly and with regularity."[14]

It was essential under the Spanish regime that the militia be maintained, trained, and armed appropriately, but reliance on the militia presented O'Reilly with a significant predicament. Militia training took men away from the fields and trades essential for the growth of the colony's economy. In contradiction to his directive for training the militia, O'Reilly ordered that militia musters be arranged so that they did not inconvenience the locals or create resentment against Spanish rule over the French population. O'Reilly's contradictory orders illustrate a paradox that would vex all ordinary and compulsory militias. Community-based militias were expected to be trained, but they were often poorly trained due to their essential obligations in the community.

Lieutenant Governor of Upper Louisiana Charles Delassus assumed control from 1799 to 1804 and maintained the previous compulsory militia companies in the main population centers of St. Louis, Ste. Genevieve, and Cape Girardeau. In December 1802 and 1803, three militia companies from Ste. Genevieve, Platin, and New Bourbon were formed into a territorial battalion for an expedition against the Native Americans in the New Madrid area.[15] The New Madrid campaign was the largest militia movement of the colonial era in Missouri.

In contrast to the French and Spanish systems, where the militia supplemented the regular army, the English colonial ordinary militia was considered a military force in its own right. The English view that a standing army could be a threat to royal authority meant that the militia played a primary, rather than a supporting, role in community defense. As the frontier moved west and the Indian threat in Missouri diminished, the militia's role in community defense contracted and the ordinary militia became dormant; their remaining role in maintaining law and order was taken over by the volunteer militia.[16]

During their colonial experience, the English learned to amalgamate separate ordinary militia units into larger bodies as needed. English "trained bands," select bodies of militia that drilled as a group, were formed in the Massachusetts Bay Colony. During the 1636 Pequot War, several trained bands were assembled into a larger unit to become the first official militia regiment in English North America.[17] As a template for future militia organizations, the English model traveled westward, transitioning into a United States model that entered the Upper Louisiana Territory in 1804.

In the citizen-soldier model, when the state required militia service, the ordinary militia became a compulsory militia for as long as needed by the state. Membership in the compulsory militia was determined by the nature of the emergency and local customs that defined the age range and the social status for service. Generally males between fifteen and sixty years were identified for compulsory service, but this assemblage included some too young and some too old for the rigors of a campaign; therefore, males between eighteen and forty-five years were most often called on for extended duty.

---

14. Billon, *Annals of St. Louis in Its Early Days*, 330–32.

15. Ibid., 318–32.

16. Boucher, "Colonial Militia as a Social Institution," 125–30.

17. Osgood, *American Colonies in the Seventeenth Century*, 1:510.

In the class-based eighteenth century, service in the English militia was a right reserved for freemen, but in French or Spanish colonial militias, especially on the frontier, slaves were often enlisted.[18] The French and Spanish both raised slave companies in the colonies, and the English colonies, out of necessity, organized slaves against Native Americans and later against colonists in the American Revolution and the War of 1812. Units of former slaves were common in the Union Army toward the end of the Civil War. The failure to tap the slave population in the South is one reason the South lost the battle of attrition with the North.

The volunteer militia was an altogether separate class of militia found in the English colonies and later American states. Members were not compelled to join the ordinary militia nor was their training limited to several muster days. Volunteers wanted an active role in community defense, preferred the company of their social peers, and had the money to purchase uniforms and better equipment. In many ways the volunteer militia, more than the ordinary militia, served an important role as a sodality, binding the community and nation together.[19] This was important for the early republic and the frontier before the advent of formal social groups that assumed this function.

Enlisting in a volunteer unit meant abiding by the bylaws of the volunteer company. If the volunteer unit was recognized by the state, they were governed by the same militia regulations as the ordinary militia in addition to their own organization's unique operating rules and regulations. When a volunteer company invested its own funds in distinctive uniforms, they were referred to as "uniform militia" or "uniform volunteer militia." In exchange for their additional time and expense, volunteers were excused from ordinary militia musters and after six years of service were excused from further militia obligation, unlike the ordinary militia requirement of ten years.[20]

In theory, the ordinary and volunteer militia complemented each other within the militia system, with volunteers filling the role of elite forces and the ordinary or compulsory militia the regular line infantry. But in practice they were often antagonistic; the state-appointed leaders of the ordinary militia complained that the volunteer militia siphoned off the best men and potential leaders from the ordinary militia, leaving the less capable and less motivated to attend musters of the ordinary militia. The volunteer leaders, in turn, often acted as though they (and not the militia as a whole) were the guardians of the state.

English ordinary colonial militias, and the state militias that followed, were restricted in movement by law and tradition within the militia company. This arrangement served well for a local defense force, but it hampered the militia as a regional offensive force. English colonial officials sought ways to circumvent customary laws prohibiting militia from moving freely. A practical solution was to avoid militia restrictions by simply calling for volunteers. Efforts to form volunteer companies began in 1634, but colonial governments feared private companies might challenge royal authority.[21] One hundred years later that fear was replaced by military necessity and volunteer companies were welcomed. Volunteers were technically not militia, but men who had volunteered from the ordinary militia; hence, they were free to cross boundaries as necessary. The need to raise troops for a mobile fighting force led to requests for more volunteers, starting a trend that would eventu-

18. Holmes, *Honor and Fidelity*, 33.
19. Laver, *Citizens More Than Solders*, 2.
20. *Laws of the State of Missouri, 1838*, 104.
21. Ibid., 497.

ally supplant the ordinary militia with an all-volunteer militia.[22] The reliance on ordinary militia in American military doctrine was over before the start of the Civil War, although it would resurface at times in the form of national service during wartime.

Volunteer militia companies are the true precursors of the modern National Guard. Although there are many similarities between the ordinary and compulsory militia, the prime distinction that separates the volunteer militia from both of those is the willingness to serve without the requirement to serve; as one historian wrote, the National Guardsman is "essentially an amateur soldier; the militiaman was ever a civilian."[23]

The armory or its equivalent structure may not have existed during the colonial periods in Missouri. The village green, common field, or town square was the militia muster and training grounds. St. Louis was laid out with a militia training ground in Block 7 on the original city plan called the Place d'Armes. Since each man supplied his own arms and accoutrements, there was little need for storage space and office requirements were minimal. During times of danger, the state paid close attention to the ordinary militia and training musters, but in peacetime both the state and militiamen tended to ignore the periodic musters.

Volunteer companies, however, continued to train in peacetime. They often drilled weekly and needed storage space for equipment and socializing; therefore an indoor facility such as an arena or hall was a necessity. In the ideal militia building, there would be some office space, a training area, equipment storage, and secure storage for stands of arms. Whereas the volunteers may have thought they were a cut above the common militia, their lasting impact on the American militia was to establish a link between a unit and a building to call home: the predecessor of the National Guard armory.

Commissioning the Militia

The Second United States Congress passed the Militia Act of 1792 to give the state militias a legal foundation after the Revolutionary War. The 1792 act remained the legal basis for the national militia organization for the next 111 years, an amazing span encompassing the change from flintlocks to bolt action rifles, from small to large armies, and from insular considerations to overseas empire.

In keeping with the English-based militia tradition, the act enshrined the principle of citizen-based defense of the United States in the state militias. Technically, for the next century every able-bodied male citizen from age eighteen to forty-five was to enroll in the ordinary militia, but the Militia Act included a long list of exemptions beginning with the United States vice president, all members of Congress, all custom-house officials and their clerks, all postmasters, ferrymen, and many more. Of special note, the Act and Missouri legislation allowed individual citizens to belong to volunteer groups, thereby fulfilling their militia obligation.[24]

The Act was never considered perfect. It had many "defects," as George Washington called them, and repeated requests for changes failed to move Congress, which was wedded to power sharing and state control of the militia. By making each state responsible for training and selecting officers, the Act assured continued inefficiency.

22. Kreidberg and Henry, *History of Military Mobilization*, 7.
23. Todd, "Our National Guard," 74.
24. *Laws of the State of Missouri, 1825*, 540.

Successive presidents, especially in times of peace, reduced the size of the regular army while placing more reliance on the state militia system for national defense. In 1802, the Jefferson adminis-tration reduced the regular army by half and enlarged the mission of the militia system, but without improving that system. The resulting national army of state citizen-soldiers, hampered by variations between the states and local inefficiencies in militia organization, was willing but unable to react to national emergencies. The War of 1812 seemed to accentuate all the failings in the militia system and find none of the positives.[25]

Aside from local Indian wars and militia responses, the status of the militia remained unchanged in the decades after the War of 1812. The situation varied from state to state, but the ordinary militia was inactive whereas the volunteer militia remained active. Just prior to the Civil War, the ordinary militia was rejuvenated in Missouri, but it split during the war when parts of the state militia and some volunteers under Missouri Governor Claiborne Fox Jackson joined the Confederacy. Other parts of the state militia and volunteer units followed the new state government under Governor Hamilton R. Gamble, which stayed with the Union.

During the turmoil following the Civil War years, the militia, ordinary and volunteer, had to be reorganized. Those men in federal service and state militias were discharged into civilian life, effec-tively decommissioning the state militia. Enlisting men and attracting prominent citizens as officers in a new Missouri militia was not an easy task in a war-weary state. After many false starts, the militia resumed in a form resembling its prewar structure. The ordinary militia returned to a dormant state, while volunteer units slowly reformed to assume the ordinary militia's law and order role.

An economic downturn in the 1870s set the stage for the Great Railroad Strike of 1877, which was compounded by a plague of locusts in Missouri and neighboring states. The labor strikes gen-erated by the depressed market hit the major cities of the east and Midwest, raising fears of class warfare. The possibility of a strike and even riots struck fear into the hearts of the middle class, and threatened the local economy.

The same concern for riot control was felt by Kansas City businessmen in 1905. To quell those fears, a 1905 Kansas City brochure proposed a battery of artillery for the city, explaining the con-nection:

> It is known by few business men that every fire insurance policy contains this clause, "This Fire Insurance Company shall not be liable for loss caused directly or indirectly by invasion, insurrec-tion, RIOT, civil war or COMMOTION."
>
> There is no doubt but that this clause cancels every dollar of fire insurance the moment a riot starts (and all cities have riots).
>
> The strongest and the best protection to the business man is the arm of the National Guard, and the value of property saved and protected by the troops in time of trouble runs up into countless millions.[26]

These fears spurred the formation of new volunteer militia units instead of the ordinary militia. Although the ordinary militia existed by law in most states, the Missouri militia was incapable of responding if called to act in an emergency. To fill this void, companies of volunteers, recruited from the middle class and officered by the social elite, stepped forward. Large and small communities in

25. Skeen, *Citizen Soldiers*, 1–3.
26. Joseph W. Folk, "Reproducing the Beautiful Kansas City Casino," Militia Folder, HSTL.

cities such as St. Louis, Carthage, and Pierce City countered labor threats with volunteers dedicated to home defense instead of national defense.

Many of the post–Civil War volunteer militia became uniform militia, paying for their own arms and equipment. This was expensive and often limited the size and composition of the company by screening out those who could not pay the price. Therefore, units sought help from the state in the matter of acquiring arms. In accordance with the Militia Act of 1792, the state militia office received arms and equipment from the federal government based on reported yearly militia rosters. These arms were to be held by the state or distributed to legally sponsored units for state defense.

As state militia offices frequently reported that the quantity of arms the federal government sent was insufficient to supply all state militia members, the federal government became more cautions about sending arms to states without accurate records of militia enrollment and careful accounting of the distribution of arms. Control of guns and cannon allowed the federal government to exert more control over the militias through the state militia office. Eventually the federal government gained control over what militias could and could not do in exchange for providing increased funding for arms and training.

The need to account for and care for arms supplied by the state increased the need for storage and meeting spaces, but most states, Missouri included, refused to provide adequate funding for proper militia facilities. The growing number of volunteer militia units and the need for secure quarters forced officials to cast about on their own for armories and the means to fund them.

The volunteer militia in various states were already called the National Guard, but these volunteer militia continued to function only at the state level until they were first called to act as a unified body in 1898 when President McKinley requested 125,000 volunteers from the state volunteer militias for the Spanish-American War. The War Department had planned on a force of sixty thousand men to prosecute the war against Spain, but political considerations forced the administration to call for a larger number. More than doubling the national military force in preparation for the war caused the federal supply bureaus to scramble for weapons and equipment. The shortages and slow pace of equipping National Guard units was a consequence of conflict between the War Department and the McKinley administration, not the inability of the volunteers to comply when called on for service.[27]

After the Spanish-American War, the proliferation of volunteer units gradually increased private and state subsidies intended for militia armories. In the larger cities, a patriotic wave of armory building would produce the most spectacular and durable armories the militia ever built in the United States, the castellated armories of the militia. The castle-like armories were the first uniform armory style and appeared predominately in major cities, with smaller versions in western cities. Many were built with a combination of state funds and private contributions, but some were built with funds raised by local subscriptions and unit fundraising.

Militia Reform

The general unfavorable reputation of the state militias in the Spanish-American War and the buildup of large reserve armies overseas contributed to a reforming movement in Congress that followed the war. European countries were adapting to new technology and creating large army

---

27. Cosmas, *An Army for Empire*, 105–20.

reserve forces, whereas the US military establishment remained centered around state militias.[28] In the early twentieth century, a series of legislative acts retired the Militia Act of 1792 and thereby transformed the militia system and the US military establishment.

Legislative acts in 1903, 1908, and 1916 changed the militia from an antiquated armed force into a true army reserve. The first step was passage of the Militia Act of 1903—known as the Dick Act for its sponsor and Ohio National Guard General Officer Charles W. Dick. The second step was the Militia Act of May 1908, often called the Second Dick Act, which was followed by the National Defense Act of 1916. Taken together, these three acts and other refinements gave the federal government greater control over the National Guard in exchange for increased federal funding to state Guard units for training and equipment; these acts and refinements are the legal basis of the modern National Guard.

The Militia Act of 1903 set the 1792 Act aside and put the volunteer militia into the lead position as the representative of the militia system, supplanting the old concept of ordinary militia. The law redefined who was a member of the National Guard by dividing the militia into two mutually exclusive bodies, the reserve militia and organized militia. The reserve militia henceforth was to be composed of all able-bodied men between the ages of eighteen and forty-five.[29] The reserve group was not required to muster periodically or train in any manner as had their predecessor, the ordinary militia. The reserve militia was a militia force in concept only. On the other hand, the organized militia, composed of volunteers, was expected to muster on a regular basis, train to US Army standards, and be prepared to be called on by the president. The federal government provided funds as an inducement to follow the new law, paying for training, modern arms, and equipment.

The National Defense Act of 1916 capped the effort that started with the Militia Act of 1903. This act required states to provide armories for Guard units and use the term "National Guard" for all federally recognized state units. A largely unnoticed aspect of the act authorized the president to call units for war without going through the state governor. This provision was incorporated into a new oath for National Guard members that gave allegiance to both the state and the president.[30] Missouri claims the honor of being the first state to comply with the provisions in the National Defense Act of 1916. On the day of passage, a Missouri regiment took the new oath and by midyear the entire Missouri National Guard had complied.[31]

In addition to organizational changes in the National Defense Act, armory design and construction were also affected. In the period between World Wars I and II, the National Guard and federal and state governments were caught up in the international modern architectural movement, and for the first time armory construction was dominated by designs that were not influenced by local tastes. Armories in the modern style were built nationwide during the Great Depression as part of government programs (especially the Works Progress Administration, or WPA) to provide jobs and put America back to work. As part of the modern architectural movement, traditional methods of construction were shunned in favor of new designs and new construction techniques. The result was a large initial wave of distinct art deco, streamline moderne, and WPA-modern style armories distributed across all states. The castellated-style armories continued to be built into the early twentieth

---

28. Ambrose, *Upton and the Army*, 109–11.
29. Militia Act of 1903 (32 Stat. 775), chaps. 195–96.
30. National Defense Act of 1916 (Pub.L. 64-85, 39 Stat. 166), sections 95 and 97.
31. Adjutant General, *Report...1915–1916*, 4.

century, but the modern style overlapped, with armories being built in that style beginning early in the twentieth century and extending into the 1970s.

With the passage of the national defense acts, the National Guard achieved its current legal form. The emergence of the Cold War out of the embers of World War II was a major factor in forging a closer relationship between the US Army and the National Guard. The US Army was drastically reduced in size, but its peacetime mission expanded.[32] The manpower for the Cold War military mission had to come from one of two reserve forces available to the US Army, the Army Reserve and the National Guard.

During the Cold War years, the Korean conflict convinced the army that National Guard training was not sufficient for the new mission. The postwar army emphasis on universal training, a period of training at regular army training schools, forced changes in cherished Guard traditions. The Guard's traditional weekly drill meetings, typically four hours long, were consolidated into one two-day weekend each month. Technically, the two-day weekend was actually four separate four-hour training periods. Therefore a two-day weekend only meant sixteen hours for pay purposes. This change was intended to use time more efficiently and allow Guard training to be more detailed and in depth. The traditional regimental training period was now a required block of two weeks a year.

In the postwar years, the new consolidated weekend drills followed a general consolidation of small units into larger units centered in larger towns. The amalgamation of units or increase in size of units in the state meant a change in armory size and location. Larger units required larger training areas, which meant a unit more frequently moved to out-of-town destinations where larger unit training occurred. Before these changes, large unit training had occurred only during the short summer training period and all other training occurred at the home armory.

The accepted method of inducting guardsmen into a company through home armory training also had to change. The Army believed the state militias' basic training led to inconsistencies in training or worse, ineffective training. State National Guard training schools were gradually eliminated and as of 1960, all inductees into the National Guard have had to complete regular US Army basic training and advanced individual training at regular army facilities.

The Cold War required the Guard to make certain sacrifices in order to become a well-trained and ready reserve for the Army. These changes had positive and negative effects on the National Guard. On the positive side, the professionalism in the Guard—dress, physical fitness, and education—increased. For a volunteer organization, this was often a big sacrifice as it took time away from the guardsman's family and full-time profession. On the negative side, the Cold War resulted in removing Guard units from the numerous small communities in Missouri; consolidation of the many small units into larger units based in fewer cities reduced the visibility of the Guard across the state.

Army-mandated changes to the traditional National Guard lifestyle caused changes in how the Guard was housed. Necessity in the post–World War II world drove the next stage of development in armory design and construction. In this case, the new armory style was far removed from the traditional castellated armory or the novel art deco and WPA-style armory. The product was a generic building—the midcentury modern, or type 783 armory—that emphasized utility. The new armory designs were examples of efficiency and cost-effectiveness taken to an extreme as the federal government dictated building design through cost control. Unfortunately for the National Guard, these armories have little curbside appeal and did little to bolster the National Guard image. Toward the

32. Blair, *Forgotten War*, 26–29.

end of the Cold War period, when corporate image was again recognized as important, the type 783 armories began to lose favor in government circles. This led to the next category in armory construction. In the late Cold War and post–Cold War periods, traditional design elements began to reappear in place of the purely functional buildings in the postmodern category.

In this study, the various periods of Missouri armory development have been divided into categories based on style and timeframe. Several of the categories match the architectural style of the armory—the castellated, the art deco and WPA, and the midcentury modern. Others—the vernacular, the postmodern, and the unique—are categories created to describe a grouping of armories. These categories facilitate providing information about the style and context to demonstrate how architectural form and historic events interact. They also show how styles transform into something visibly new in response to changing historical needs.

The categories are arranged chronologically to avoid unintended evaluations about the worth of one armory style over another. The six categories are: vernacular, castellated, art deco and WPA, midcentury modern, postmodern, and unique. Each category is coupled with a descriptive historical label that connects the style to a historical period.

vernacular	main street armories
castellated	castle armories
art deco and WPA	Depression-era armories
midcentury modern	type 783 armories
postmodern	traditional revival armories
unique	architectural gems

For each armory style, numerous photographs are included. The captions include the name of the armory, the style, the location, the dates of use, and the name of the architect or builder, if known. For later armories, the date of use is the same as the date of construction/dedication. Earlier armories, the vernacular or reuse buildings, may have a different construction date from that of militia/National Guard occupancy.

Chapter 2
Main Street Armories
The Vernacular Category

During the French colonial period in Missouri, towns like Ste. Genevieve and St. Louis each had a *place d'armes* analogous to Jackson Square in New Orleans, the primary capital of French Louisiana.[1] In French custom, the square was a central location between the river and the town, and was the area used for required militia musters. In addition to drilling the company when the militia was mustered on the square, the commanding officer was required to complete an attendance roll and handle other company business. In the early colonial days, a company's headquarters might have been under a shade tree or in a local home, or after more development, in an official building or a public house.

As colonial towns prospered and grew, local businesses and families built a variety of structures, from shacks to mansions, that the militia could use to hold musters and attend to important paperwork and company matters in a convenient shelter away from the elements. Before and after the Louisiana Purchase in 1804, new communities on the frontier often gathered at the house of the local militia captain. It was during the American period of control in the Louisiana colony that the earliest recorded meeting of a Missouri volunteer militia took place in 1808 at the St. Louis home owned by Italian immigrant Emelien Yosti, on the corner of Main (First Street) and Locust Streets.[2] Yosti was a businessman, trader, and tavern keeper who provided refreshments on muster days. Another early recorded meeting of a frontier militia took place in central Missouri at the small river town of Franklin, when the Franklin Dragoons assembled in 1819 at the house of W. V. Rector, probably the captain of the militia unit.[3]

Sometime after the early American period in Missouri, a change occurred in the traditional outdoor muster and social gathering. Instead of meeting wherever the militia captain chose, a new tradition arose where the militia met indoors at a set location. For the militia, this was a simple move from an outdoor setting to a building rented for musters, but it was a monumental shift from the established order. As American militias adjusted to the new tradition and sought places for indoor meetings, their first option was to rent a commercial space, usually a building of vernacular construction. The vernacular style is the oldest and most common style of architecture used for armories in Missouri.

---

1. Primm, *Lion of the Valley*, 15.
2. Hyde and Conard, *Encyclopedia of History of St. Louis*, 2566.
3. "Franklin Dragoons," *Missouri Intelligencer*, May 21, 1819.

Fig. 2.1: Bequet-Ribault House, Ste. Genevieve, 2001. French *poteaux en terre*, built late eighteenth century. This building is similar in style to the Yosti building. (Photo: Wiegers)

Vernacular architecture is often called Americana, common, or traditional because it lacks a defining architectural style. A vernacular building is not by definition devoid of ornamentation, but features associated with high-style architecture are more chance applications than intentional choices, since this style of building is the product of the builder's art, not the creation of a professional architect. There were many unknown carpenter-practitioners who built and widely disseminated the vernacular style. Instead of building with stone, marble, or brick associated with an accepted style, vernacular-style buildings are constructed with local materials, most often wood.

Without a beginning point, associated style, or architects to promote it, the vernacular is recognized but not well understood, and definitions of the style vary widely. The word "vernacular" was not associated with architectural styles until 1964 when Bernard Rudofsky borrowed it from linguistic studies of local or regional dialects and applied it to architecture in an exhibit at the Museum of Modern Art in New York. Rudofsky describes vernacular architecture as "anonymous, spontaneous, indigenous, rural."[4] A working definition of the vernacular style is "a type of architecture that emphasizes the intimate relationship between everyday objects and culture, between ordinary buildings and people."[5] The word "common" is often used to describe vernacular architecture, but the word is not meant in a negative manner; rather it refers to the way everyday people build for various purposes. Using speech as an analogy to architecture, colloquial speech is the opposite of formal speech, just as vernacular architecture is the opposite of classical architectural style.

Vernacular-type buildings used as armories before the advent of modern armories can be found in a stroll down any small-town main street. Likely candidates are those with a commercial front, factory space, or large covered area; it may have a wood, brick, or prefabricated metal front. Most of

4. Rudofsky, *Architecture without Architects*, 1.
5. Carter and Cromley, *Invitation to Vernacular Architecture*, 7–8.

the vernacular armory buildings can be classified as one-part and two-part commercial blocks. The one-part is a single story, a box in shape with a decorated façade.[6] The two-part commercial block is simply a one-part commercial block placed on top of another, forming a two- to four-story building. The primary characteristic of the two-part commercial block is the horizontal division between the ground and upper levels. The ground floor is a work area, whereas the second or higher floors are activity zones for large or small functions and residential use.[7] For instance, the Fayette Opera House is a three-part commercial block; it had storefronts on the ground floor and the upper two floors were devoted to the opera stage and seating, and a few offices.

Fig. 2.2: Vernacular armory at Unionville, Missouri, 1994 (Photo: Wiegers)

The typical armory storefront building may have one to three stories, with a narrow front and deep lot. Interior arrangement may vary from one or two large rooms to several smaller rooms. Larger cities were not exceptions from the trend of vernacular building, but in the course of real estate development, large cities were more likely to replace the common architecture of the frontier and early settlement periods with buildings of later architectural styles. If a typical militia unit of 1840 were to have described its ideal armory, the unit would probably have wished for a structure like a riding arena or exposition hall such as Armory Hall in St. Louis. An ideal hall would have had a high ceiling and open space for large-unit infantry training and cavalry movements, as well as some space for secure storage and administrative offices. Most militiamen would have assumed the building would be a simple design with four corners and peaked roof, probably built of wood with few embellishments.

Money was the primary factor preventing rural units from building large armory halls. The small allowance the state allocated to the militia provided little for rent money, and was hardly enough to consider purchasing a building. The issue of building rental illustrates a dichotomy between urban and rural militia units. Larger cities had a much better chance of attracting a generous patron to help

6. Longstreth, *Main Street*, 54–55.

7. Ibid., 24.

with rent money, whereas smaller cities and towns had a smaller pool of wealth to draw from. The issue of the availability of suitable space, however, tended to equalize town and country Guard units. A small-town Guard unit had fewer options from which to choose for a rented armory, because most small towns prior to the 1900s lacked large indoor spaces of the size needed. Large cities had the reverse problem with space: there were more suitable spaces available in the city, but also more competition vying for the same large space.

Reduced to its most essential function, the vernacular armory was little more than a shelter from the elements. A focus on this basic function matched the attitude of the ordinary militia as the most basic of soldiery. Most members assembled for musters because they were required to under penalty of law; hence they were present for the moment and, once dismissed, were gone until the next mandatory drill. Few cared if it was raining or snowing except that it increased their discomfort and limited the extent of unit maneuvers. Drill muster was mandatory, hence not a day to take seriously.[8]

This nonchalant attitude toward militia service spurred the rise of the volunteer militia and brought a degree of professionalism to the militia and its training. Insofar as the development of the armory is concerned, volunteers, by virtue of their commitment to preparedness, needed a building for training and storage. The transition from *place d'armes* meetings of compulsory militia to an armory building rented or constructed by volunteers was born out of state frugality. The Missouri legislature did not provide adequate funds to support the militia and the state did not provide funds to build a unit armory until the 1880s.[9]

Since volunteer militia members often purchased their own uniforms and arms, they needed a building with storage space. Storing arms and equipment presented two concerns for all militia. Weapons had a high value due to their scarcity and were easily stolen, so to prevent theft and maintain accountability for weapons and equipment, Guard units needed a secure storage system or arms room. In addition, units had to maintain the arms, whether their own or state-provided, in storage spaces that were not climate controlled, which meant an ongoing battle with dirt and rust. To counter this problem, an armorer was hired to clean, repair, and oil each piece throughout the year. According to some accounts, the connection between a home for the militia and location of maintenance of the militia's arms led to the serendipitous attachment of the term "armory" to the militia home.[10]

The vexing problem of securing arms and ammunition reached a crescendo as late as 1935 during congressional testimony before the Committee on Military Affairs. A combined subcommittee report from the Committee on Military Affairs estimated that approximately $150 million worth of federal property was being stored with the National Guard, and newspapers frequently published stories of rifles, ammunition, and machine guns being stolen.[11] Hearings before the subcommittees on this matter illuminated the poor condition of many state armories. National Guard units were often housed in temporary buildings or in the second and third stories of office buildings and businesses, as they had been since the beginning of the Republic. It was obvious to the committee that home-built lockers and arms racks did not protect the high-value contents of such armories.

---

8. Bek, "Followers of Duden," 362–67.

9. Hyde and Conard, *Encyclopedia of History of St. Louis*, 38–39.

10. Ibid., 38.

11. US Congress, Senate, *Joint Hearing ... Construction of National Guard Armories* (1935), 3.

Much to the embarrassment of the National Guard, local authorities reported that over 2,047 firearms and 273,326 rounds of ammunition had been stolen from armories between January 1, 1933, and October 28, 1935. Not all of these thefts were attributed to shoddy, rented buildings with poor security. Other forces, such as organized crime, were also at work; as one reporter observed, "The underworld steals its heavier weapons and purchases its pistols."[12]

Storage for equipment other than arms was another concern for volunteer companies, due to the numerous changes of clothing and small items each guardsman had to keep available. In the 1890s, one individual would have been issued one campaign hat, two blue shirts, two sets of underwear, socks, one coat, one pair of trousers, army shoes, one blanket, a haversack, a ration can, a tin cup, knife, fork, and spoon, a rifle, a cartridge belt, and half of a two-man tent.[13] When this list of basic items is multiplied by one hundred men, it is easy to appreciate the problem companies faced in providing secure storage.

Often militia units found themselves renting quarters that were at odds with their military image. In St. Louis, the militia often found the cheapest, but not always the most suitable, accommodations on a second-floor hayloft over horse stables. The prestigious St. Louis Greys were located on the second floor of Thornton's stable; the Washington Guards were over Lee and Rucker's stable; and the ethnic German units found space in their Turnverein Halls. Companies often became so associated with a specific building that their association changed the building identity. Verandah Hall, for instance, located at Fourth and Washington Streets in St. Louis, became known as Armory Hall (see fig. 2.47).[14] One Columbia Guard unit was renting a former church building as late as 1910. Their armory boasted stained glass cathedral windows and a short, brick bell tower that contrasted noticeably with the sign over the door proclaiming it to be the home of "Co. G, 4th Infantry, N.G.Mo." (National Guard of Missouri; see fig. 2.3).[15]

As volunteer units acquired or rented higher quality quarters that matched their unit pride, it became necessary to find a more regular income to pay for that better quality. Thus the armory building acquired a new mission: it had to be a moneymaker in addition to a drill hall, arms depot, and central place to socialize and recruit members. In 1857, the St. Louis Washington Guards required $1,000 a year for building rental.[16] Renting out the spacious drill hall for civic and private events covered all or most of the mortgage and the unit's operating expenses. At a time when most cities had few if any large public meeting halls, the volunteer militia hall became the neighborhood place to congregate for theatre productions, charity events, political rallies, private parties, and emergencies. Community use of militia halls became so common that in the 1960s musical *The Music Man*, fast-talking salesman Harold Hill noted that the young folks were "Headin' for the dance at the Arm'ry!"

Not all private armories proved to be adequate for militia purposes. One privately owned building in Kansas City that was leased to the state in 1910 was deficient in drill space and poorly maintained. It also lacked sufficient space for storing equipment.[17] Guard units, especially those in big cities, commonly complained that rents were too high for single company armories and that the

12. "Heavy Military Arms are Stolen by Gang," *New York Times*, October 29, 1935.

13. "First Missouri Volunteers," [newspaper unknown] 1890s, Newspaper clippings file, MMMH.

14. Ibid.

15. Adjutant General, *Biennial Report...1909–1910*, 81, pl. 53.

16. Constitution, Minutes of the Washington Guards, December 4, 1857, National Guard Collection, Constitution of Washington Guards folder, SHS MO–St. Louis.

17. Division of Militia Affairs, *Report...1910*, 119.

larger buildings suitable for multiple units were chronically in short supply.[18] The obvious step was for each Guard unit to build a suitable armory, but such an option was only a possibility for the wealthiest units.

The housing situation remained dire for most volunteer units. A 1912 report on armories nationwide listed all of the problems militia units had encountered in the previous hundred years. Of all US armories, 26 percent did not have drill halls large enough to facilitate indoor instruction of a single company. Almost 10 percent of unit commanders said nonmilitary use of the armory facility (i.e., renting out the armory for civilian events) impeded unit training. The report found 32 percent of all armories to be "ill sited," poorly constructed, and underequipped, and noted that 10 percent failed to provide protection for government property, which included everything from rifles to knapsacks.[19]

According to Captain C. E. Fowler of Kennett, his armory in 1935 was lacking the basic armory facilities.

Fig. 2.3: Former Methodist Church, Columbia, Missouri, converted to an armory in 1910 for Company G, Fourth Infantry, 1909 (Photo from Miller, "Columbia Methodism")

The present armory has been disapproved by every inspecting officer who has visited this unit in the last six years. The present armory is not equipped with running water, toilet nor bath facilities, nor fire extinguishers, and is located in the second story over two dry goods stores. The building is extremely hazardous because of not having any fire exits, a narrow stairway providing the only entrance to the building. The drill hall is entirely too small for practical purposes, and has a row of posts through the center of same.[20]

Insights into the volunteers' lives can be gleaned from the structure of the rented armory. A rented vernacular armory indicates that most members believed militia service was a duty rather than a

18. Adjutant General, *Report . . . 1905*, 22–23.

19. Division of Militia Affairs, *Report . . . 1912*, 46.

20. Captain C. E. Fowler, "140th Infantry Kennett Armory Report," November 16, 1935, Kennett Armory folder, MMMH.

requirement. Most probably had a higher level of education than the compulsory militia reflected in their pursuit of vigorous training. Most volunteers had a trade or professional status that allowed them to spend time and money on training and arms. Each member probably pledged to be responsible for financial support of the unit and its armory. The location of the armory on or near the town square reflects both transportation by horse and the urban housing pattern of most members.

The state's failure to support its citizen-soldiers by providing basic quarters meant that Missouri Guard commanders did not realistically expect a state-owned armory, a situation that did not change until the twentieth century. Out of necessity, commanders were forced to rely on their own wiles and initiative to solve the housing issue. The preferred solution for most commanders was to find a group of patriotic and wealthy citizens to back the cause. A respected and well-connected local base of support could provide the impetus for new armory construction to benefit the town and unit. But in most small towns, finding a group of patriotic citizens was easier than finding citizens both patriotic and wealthy.

The alternative was to locate cheap rooms that could be modified to suit Guard purposes, and vernacular buildings could fit the need for usable, affordable space. Every town square was surrounded by vernacular architecture, typically a two-story red brick commercial building. But the availability of building space did not dictate easy rental. Most often the rent exceeded the small allotment the state supplied for that purpose, leaving the company commander with three choices: do without an armory, be resigned to a substandard building or rooms, or make up the difference from private sources.

Vernacular buildings generally fit the basic needs of early volunteer militias and reflected the accepted view of defense as a civilian-based activity. Numerous examples of vernacular armories still stand and exemplify several characteristics of the National Guard: longevity, adaptability, and community support. In the context of the times, vernacular architecture served the Guard well and surviving buildings continue to be markers of Guard presence in the cityscape of America. Today, even though some Main Street armories are still in rented buildings, they are probably not adequate armories for the modern role of the National Guard. In the current age of mass marketing and brand recognition, most current vernacular armories do not convey the Guard image expected of successful corporate architecture.

Early Armory Buildings in Missouri

The history behind each armory building is tied to a social problem and a solution. In frontier times, the militia was a local institution that mirrored the transplanted European social order, selecting militia leaders from elected officials and the educated class rather than from a hereditary elite. As an arm of the state, the militia was not inordinately centralized nor was it dominated by a body of warriors. Its leadership cadre was small and dominated by local experts. This homespun governance allowed regional tastes to dominate in decisions about using vernacular buildings for militia purposes. The armory building, if there was one in a frontier town, would have reflected local preferences in commercial and residential building styles.

In frontier communities in Missouri, where a militia's primary responsibilities were related to its position on the border between European American and Native American cultures, militia units had little cause for a home until later generations of militia found their responsibilities expanded. As the pressure for a permanent home increased, militia leaders were obliged to rent and often erect their own buildings to provide space for drill and storage, and to provide the unit with an identity. Although it was the state's responsibility to provide for all militia needs, including shelter, the state rarely provided enough to rent adequate accommodations and companies had to make do with available funds or find ways to raise additional funds. The early emphasis on making do with little support became a hallmark of the National Guard. Paying rent for the use of a vernacular building as an armory fostered a tradition of self-help in volunteer units that is still found in many Guard units.

The major sources of information on early armory buildings are the periodic/biennial reports of the adjutant general (the 1909–1910 report included a partial survey of armories with photographs taken in 1909), The Guard's *Historical Annual* of 1939 (which included another survey of armories and some photographs), and photographs from the Missouri National Guard Facilities Engineers office and the collection at the Museum of Missouri Military History.

Inventory of Main Street Armory Buildings (by date built)

Fig. 2.4: Pierce City 1890 Armory (just left of center with peaked roof), ca. 1890
Walnut Street, Pierce City, Lawrence County
Style: vernacular
Built ca. 1840; occupied by Guard ca. 1890
Architect/builder unknown
Photo: MMMH

Fig. 2.5: Turnverein Hall/former Company B, Third Infantry Armory, 1997
518 Vine Street, Boonville, Cooper County
Style: German vernacular
Built 1847; occupied by Guard ca. 1913
Architect/builder unknown
Photo: Chuck MacFall

Fig. 2.6: Former Washington Hall Armory, 1944
SW corner Third and Elm Streets, St. Louis
Style: commercial vernacular
Built ca. 1850; occupied by Guard ca. 1861
Builder: George Schneider
Photo: J. Orville Speen Papers, WHMC

Fig. 2.7: Company A, Fourth Infantry Armory, 1909

Main Street, Tarkio, Atchison County

Style: Italianate commercial

Built ca. 1860; occupied by Guard by 1909

Architect/builder unknown

Photo from *Biennial Report of the Adjutant General 1909–1910*

Fig. 2.8: Commercial bank/former Company B, Third Infantry Armory, 1994

400 Main Street, Boonville, Cooper County

Style: Missouri German vernacular

Built ca. 1860; occupied by Guard 1925 26

Architect/builder unknown

Photo: Chuck MacFall

Fig. 2.9: Robertson Property/former Battery D, 203rd Coast Artillery Armory, 1997
Sixth and Morgan Streets, Boonville, Cooper County
Style: German vernacular
Built ca. 1870; occupied by Guard ca. 1923
Architect/builder unknown
Photo: Chuck MacFall

The Robertson Property, also called "the stables," may have been a convenient rental when the Boonville Guard acquired horses, caissons, and cannon. The building is still in commercial use.

Fig. 2.10: Macomb Building/Company C, Second Infantry Armory, 1909
804–808 First Street, Lamar, Barton County
Style: three-story commercial block
Built before 1885; occupied by Guard as early as 1896–at least 1916
Architect/builder unknown
Photo from *Biennial Report of the Adjutant General 1909–1910*

Fig. 2.11: McLaughlin Building/former Battery D, 203rd Coast Artillery Armory, 1997
505 Main Street, Boonville, Cooper County
Style: German vernacular
Built ca. 1890; occupied by Guard ca. 1923
Architect/builder unknown
Photo: Chuck MacFall

The second floor of this building was an armory in 1923. This building was one of many short-term armories to serve the Boonville Guard in the early 1900s. The building is in commercial use.

Fig. 2.12: Headquarters Company, 175th Military Police Battalion Armory, ca. 1950
113 and 115 West Fifth Street, Fulton, Callaway County
Style: commercial vernacular block
Built ca. 1890; occupied by Guard ca. 1950
Architect/builder unknown
Photo: 175th Military Police Battalion Records, Armory file, MMMH

Fig. 2.13: Former Missouri National Guard Headquarters/former Battery A, 203rd Coast Artillery Armory, 1998

Commerce Street, Pierce City, Lawrence County

Style: three-story commercial block

Built 1890; occupied by Guard 1921–ca. 1930

Architect/builder unknown

Photo: John Viessman

At one time, this opera house was the state National Guard headquarters. This three-story, brick, row commercial building was constructed about 1890, with commercial storefronts on the first floor, offices or living quarters on the second floor, and a large open room on the third level. The tall parapet had a stamped metal cornice in the center on which were found raised letters spelling "OPERA HALL." On the narrow band of brick between the second and third story row of windows were painted letters spelling "ARMORY." Above this in smaller letters was the designation of a later unit, "BTR'Y A 203rd COAST ABT GA AD." The adjutant general at the time, William A. Raupp, began his military career in this area and moved the state headquarters to Pierce City in 1921. This historic building and the majority of downtown Pierce City were totally destroyed by a tornado in the spring of 2003.

Fig. 2.14: Hall Building/former Company D, Fourth Infantry Armory, 1909
Street address unknown, Trenton, Grundy County
Style: two-story commercial block
Built ca. 1890; occupied by Guard by 1909 (no longer standing)
Architect/builder unknown
Photo from *Biennial Report of the Adjutant General 1909–1910*

Fig. 2.15: Company F, Sixth Infantry Armory, 1909
546 High Street (?), Jackson, Cape Girardeau County
Style: commercial vernacular
Built before 1895; occupied by Guard possibly as early as 1901–at least 1909

(demolished before 1921)
Architect/builder unknown
Photo from *Biennial Report of the Adjutant General 1909–1910*

Fig. 2.16: Former Band Section, 140th Infantry Armory, 1998
105 South Main, Chaffee, Scott County
Style: two-story commercial block
Built ca. 1900; occupied by Guard ca. 1921
Architect/builder unknown
Photo: Chuck MacFall

Fig. 2.17: Independent Order of Odd Fellows (IOOF) Hall/former Booneville Armory, 1997

521 Main Street, Boonville, Cooper County

Style: two-story commercial block

Built ca. 1900; occupied by Guard ca. 1923

Architect/builder unknown

Photo: Chuck MacFall

Fig. 2.18: Former Headquarters Battery 128th Field Artillery Armory, 1994

120 South Eighth Street, Columbia, Boone County

Style: two-story commercial block

Built ca. 1900; occupied by Guard 1924–1938

Architect/builder unknown

Photo: Wiegers

The top floor of the structure was used as an armory from 1924 to 1938. According to a 1936 city directory, a business named Benedict's Garage used the bottom portion of the two-story building.[21] The 128th Field Artillery drilled on the top floor until 1938, when the unit moved into a new art deco/WPA armory at 701 East Ash Street. The building is still in commercial use.

Fig. 2.19: Service Battery, 128th Field Artillery Armory, 1939

Main Street, Burlington Junction, Nodaway County

Style: parapet commercial block

Built ca. 1900; occupied by Guard ca. 1939 (no longer standing)

Architect/builder unknown

Photo from *Historical Annual, 1939*

21. *City Directory: Columbia, Mo. and Boone County*, 1936, SHS MO.

Fig. 2.20: Former Battery A, 129th Field Artillery Armory, ca. 1950
127 Main Street, Clinton, Henry County
Style: two-story commercial block
Built ca. 1900; occupied by Guard ca. 1937
Architect/builder unknown
Photo: MMMH

Fig. 2.21: Former Band Section, 140th Infantry Armory, 1997

145 West Yoakum Street, Chaffee, Scott County

Style: commercial vernacular

Built ca. 1900; occupied by Guard ca. 1936

Architect/builder unknown

Photo: Chuck MacFall

Fig. 2.22: White Eagle Dairy/former Headquarters and Headquarters Battery, 128th Field Artillery Armory, 1993

112 South Eighth Street, Columbia, Boone County

Style: two-story commercial block

Built ca. 1900; occupied by Guard ca. 1923

Architect/builder unknown

Photo: Chuck MacFall

Fig. 2.23: Boone Building/former Company G, Fourth Infantry Armory, 1997

617 East Broadway, Columbia, Boone County

Style: three-story commercial block

Built 1900; occupied by Guard 1913–1914

Architect/builder unknown

Photo: Chuck MacFall

This building was occupied by the Guard around May 1913. It was an improvement over their previous building because it had steam heat, phone service, and "shower bath(s)."[22] The unit remained in this building until January 1914, when the Independent Order of Odd Fellows (IOOF) leased the third floor of the Boone Building. The building was razed circa 1998.

Fig. 2.24: O'Rear Building/former Battery B, First Artillery Armory, 1997

921 East Broadway, Columbia, Boone County

Style: three-story commercial block

Built ca. 1900; occupied by Guard 1920–1922

Architect/builder unknown

Photo: Chuck MacFall

This building, originally constructed with three stories, was drastically modified when the upper one and a half floors were removed sometime after the Guard moved out.

Fig. 2.25: Company C, 135th Tank Battalion Armory, ca. 1950

Ninth and Poplar Streets, Lamar, Barton County

Style: vernacular

Built ca. 1900; occupied by Guard ca. 1950

Architect/builder unknown

Photo: MMMH

22. "Now Capt. Sebastion," *Columbia Daily Tribune*, May 1, 1913, 4.

Fig. 2.26: E. H. Bess Building/Company M, Sixth Infantry Armory, 1909
201–202 East Main, Fredericktown, Madison County
Style: commercial vernacular
Built after 1900; occupied by Guard by 1908–before 1914
Architect/builder unknown
Photo from *Biennial Report of the Adjutant General 1909–1910*

Fig. 2.27: Former Fredericktown National Guard Armory, 1997
125 South Mine LaMotte, Fredericktown, Madison County
Style: commercial vernacular
Built ca. 1900; occupied by Guard ca. 1916
Architect/builder unknown
Photo: Latham Scott

Fig. 2.28: Third Regiment Infantry Armory, 1909
Michigan Avenue at East 14th Street (?), Kansas City, Jackson County
Style: vernacular
Built ca. 1900; occupied by Guard by 1909 to ca. 1940 (no longer standing)
Architect/builder unknown
Photo from *Biennial Report of the Adjutant General 1909–1910*

Fig. 2.29: Leong Building/Company E, Fourth Infantry Armory, 1909
605 Broadway, Hannibal, Marion County
Style: commercial vernacular
Built 1900; occupied by Guard by 1909–at least 1913
Architect/builder unknown
Photo from *Biennial Report of the Adjutant General 1909–1910*

Fig. 2.30: Sandford and Walker Building/Company F, Second Infantry Armory, 1909
Street address unknown, Joplin, Jasper County
Style: commercial vernacular
Built ca. 1900; occupied by Guard ca. 1909 (no longer standing)
Architect/builder unknown
Photo from *Biennial Report of the Adjutant General 1909–1910*

Fig. 2.31: Former 735th Ordnance Company Armory, 2006
530 East State Street, Jefferson City, Cole County
Style: parapet vernacular
Built ca. 1900; occupied by Guard 1945–1952
Architect/builder unknown
Photo: MMMH

This building was constructed around 1900 to house the Missouri State Penitentiary broom warehouse.[23] In 1940, the building was used as the quartermaster warehouse for the Missouri National Guard. Between 1945 and 1952, it was occupied by the 735th Ordnance Company and utilized as office space and storage for the Missouri National Guard Quartermaster.[24] The building is currently in commercial use.

23. Ref. no. 007, 530 East State Street, Architectural/Historic Inventory Survey Form, Jefferson City Historic East, MO SHPO.
24. "Quartermaster Warehouse Centralizes Handling of Supplies, Equipment."

Fig. 2.32: Company B, Fourth Infantry Armory, 1909

202 South 17th Street, Unionville, Putnam County

Style: two-story commercial block

Built ca. 1900; occupied by Guard ca. 1909

Architect/builder unknown

Photo from *Biennial Report of the Adjutant General 1909–1910*

Fig. 2.33: Light Battery B Armory, 1909
1728 Highland, Kansas City, Jackson County
Style: commercial vernacular
Built ca. 1900; occupied by Guard ca. 1905–1925
Architect/builder unknown
Photo from *Biennial Report of the Adjutant General 1909–1910*

Future president Harry S. Truman experienced his first taste of military life when he joined Light Battery A on June 14, 1905, the same day the battery was mustered into service. This armory is probably the first armory Private Truman drilled at with the unit. It was built for the field artillery adjacent to a city park called the "Parade," which was owned by the Parade Real Estate and Building Company of Kansas City.[25] The armory was severely damaged in 1913 when an explosion occurred in a neighboring storage building. Sometime during the 1920s, the armory and outbuildings were razed.[26]

25. Adjutant General, *Biennial Report ... 1911–1912*, 42.
26. "Powder and Oil Explode," *Kansas City Times*, October 2, 1913, 1.

Fig. 2.34: Oak Street Armory, ca. 1950

1528 Oak Street, Kansas City, Jackson County

Style: two-story commercial block

Built ca. 1900; occupied by Guard ca. 1950

Architect/builder unknown

Photo: MMMH

Fig. 2.35: Upjohn Building/Headquarters Thirty-fifth Division Armory, ca. 1959

25 East Pershing Road, Kansas City, Jackson County

Style: three-story commercial block

Built ca. 1900; occupied by Guard ca. 1959

Architect/builder unknown

Photo: MMMH

Fig. 2.36: Broadway Armory, ca. 1950
1915 Broadway, Kansas City, Jackson County
Style: vernacular
Built ca. 1900; occupied by Guard ca. 1950
Architect/builder unknown
Photo: MMMH

Fig. 2.37: Company I, 138th Infantry Armory, 1939
Street address unknown, Marshall, Saline County
Style: false-front theater
Built ca. 1900; occupied by Guard ca. 1939 (no longer standing)
Architect/builder unknown
Photo from *Historical Annual*, 1939

Fig. 2.38: Company F, Fourth Infantry Armory, 1909
Third Street between Main and Buchanan, Maryville, Nodaway County
Style: two-story commercial block
Built ca. 1900; occupied by Guard ca. 1909
Architect/builder unknown
Photo from *Biennial Report of the Adjutant General 1909–1910*

Fig. 2.39: Former Company F Armory, 2000

104 & 106 Jackson Street, Perryville, Perry County

Style: two-story commercial block

Built ca. 1900; occupied by Guard ca. 1947

Architect/builder unknown

Photo: Wiegers

Fig. 2.40: Company B, Sixth Infantry Armory, 1909
423–24 St. Joseph Street, Perryville, Perry County
Style: two-story commercial block
Built ca. 1900; occupied by Guard ca. 1909
Architect/builder unknown
Photo from *Biennial Report of the Adjutant General 1909–1910*

Fig. 2.41: Company C, Sixth Infantry Armory, 1909
138 Washington Street (?), Ste. Genevieve, Ste. Genevieve County
Style: false-front commercial
Built ca. 1900; occupied by Guard ca. 1909 (no longer standing)
Architect/builder unknown
Photo from *Biennial Report of the Adjutant General 1909–1910*

Fig. 2.42: Field Hospital Armory, 1909
Olive and 12th Street, St. Joseph, Buchanan County
Style: Italianate vernacular
Built ca. 1900; occupied by Guard ca. 1909
Architect: Ben Trunk / Builder: George & Burnett
Photo from *Biennial Report of the Adjutant General 1909–1910*

Fig. 2.43: Bascom Brothers Building/Company F, Third Infantry Armory, 1909
823–824 South Main Street, Independence, Clay County
Style: commercial vernacular
Built ca. 1900; occupied by Guard by 1907–before 1917
Architect/builder unknown
Photo from *Biennial Report of the Adjutant General 1909–1910*

Fig. 2.44: Company A, Sixth Infantry Armory, 1909

303–304 Washington Ave. (?), West Plains, Howell County

Style: two-story commercial block

Built after 1900; occupied by Guard ca. 1909 (additional space in a wooden building on Main Street)

Architect/builder unknown

Photo from *Biennial Report of the Adjutant General 1909–1910*

Fig. 2.45: Service Battery, 203rd Coast Artillery Armory, 1939

200–211 Madison Ave., Aurora, Lawrence County

Style: vernacular

Built before 1902; occupied by Guard by 1902–at least 1939 (remodeled for theater use in 1914)

Architect/builder unknown

Photo from *Historical Annual,* 1939

Fig. 2.46: Clements Building/Company H, Fourth Infantry Armory, 1909

112/114 North Third Street, Louisiana, Pike County

Style: three-and-a-half-story commercial block

Built before 1902; occupied by Guard by 1909–at least 1917

Architect/builder unknown

Photo from *Biennial Report of the Adjutant General 1909–1910*

Fig. 2.47: Fayette Opera House/future Company H, 138th Infantry Armory, 1905
100 South Main Street, Fayette, Howard County
Style: three-story commercial block
Built 1905; occupied by Guard ca. 1922–1941
Architect/builder: W. J. Megraw
Photo: postcard, author's personal collection

The Fayette Opera House offered a Guard unit ample room and a source of rental income. This large, three-story brick building served for many years as the armory for Company H and later Company M, 138th Infantry.

The first floor commercial bays have been greatly altered, but the second and third floors remain intact. A large staircase from a second floor side entrance to street level provided easy access to the drill hall. The façade has a smaller entry and staircase to the second floor offices.

The building was completed in 1905 by local builder W. J. Megraw to replace a previous opera house that burned in 1902. The National Guard rented the second and third floors for a drill hall from the 1920s to early 1941 when the unit was federalized prior to World War II. The large open space on the second floor stage and seating area attracted the Guard unit to the building. The unit removed the stage and all seating, creating a large open area for unit exercise. The unit also set up a small-caliber shooting range to allow indoor practice with their water-cooled machine guns adapted to fire subcaliber rounds against the back wall. The balcony area was closed in and converted to unit storage, and the third floor held unit offices. During most weekly drills, the unit trained and marched around the town square, but during inclement weather, it trained inside.[27]

Typical of most small-town units, the Fayette Guard rented out its large open area for civic functions, dances, and special occasions. The open area served two important functions for the Guard: it helped to pay the rent on the armory space, typically more than supplied by the state, and it brought the community closer to the unit as it hosted non-Guard activities. The building is today in commercial use.

27. "Old Opera House Holds Much Fayette History," *Fayette Advertiser*, September 4, 2002.

Fig. 2.48: Patee Market/former Fourth Infantry Headquarters Armory, 1993
904 South 10th Street, St. Joseph, Buchanan County
Style: commercial pavilion
Built 1906; occupied by Guard ca. 1909
Architect/builder unknown
Photo: Chuck MacFall

Fig. 2.49: Company C, Fourth Infantry Armory, 1909
120 E. Washington Street, Kirksville, Adair County
Style: three-story commercial block
Built after 1906; occupied by Guard by 1909–at least 1914
Architect/builder unknown
Photo from *Biennial Report to the Adjutant General 1909–1910*

Fig. 2.50: Company G, Second Infantry Armory, 1909

Olive and Locust Streets, Aurora, Lawrence County

Style: commercial vernacular

Built 1907; occupied by Guard 1907–ca. 1945

Architect/builder unknown

Photo from *Biennial Report of the Adjutant General 1909–1910*

The Aurora Opera House Armory was built by its home unit, Company G, Second Infantry, National Guard of Missouri. The armory/theatre was privately owned by the Armory Theatre Association, formed to build a new armory and to replace a previous town opera house that closed in 1907. The unit chose the site of a burned hotel to build its new home and to provide the town with an opera house, a progressive social element common in all modern twentieth-century towns.[28]

This structure was designed to serve as an armory on drill days once a week and a theatre during the remaining time. In this manner the Armory Theatre Association paid for the building without soliciting funds from the community. The floor plan had limitations as both an armory and a theater. For drills, the unit had to remove the chairs and false floor, and the theater had little room to store its equipment when the hall was being used for popular athletic events.

The theatre was later remodeled into one of Aurora's first "motion picture houses." The front and interior were remodeled again in 1935 and renamed the Princess. The façade and arcade appear to have a modern style in vogue at the time that remained until the theatre burned in February 1943.

The supply platoon and "Houn' Dawg" band of the 203rd Coast Artillery, both Aurora units, were mobilized from the armory/theatre on September 16, 1940. During their absence, a new armory was built in the modern/art deco style. The theatre was sold sometime in the postwar period and was remodeled again, but is still called the Princess.[29]

28. Aurora Centennial Committee, *Aurora Centennial, 1870–1970: Yesterday and Today,* 5.

29. Ibid.

Fig. 2.51: Standard Oil Building/Building #1, Administration Building, former Headquarters and Headquarters Company, 135th Signal Battalion Armory, 1997

Ninth and Monterey Streets, St. Joseph, Buchanan County

Style: vernacular

Built 1908; occupied by Guard 1955–1988

Architect/builder: J. Kay Cleavinger

Photo: Chuck MacFall

The Standard Oil home office in St. Joseph, Missouri, was at one time the headquarters of the 135th Signal Battalion. The armory is actually a compound of five buildings arranged around a rectangular courtyard. Building #1 was the main administrative area, Building #2 was used as an organizational maintenance shop, Building #3 was used for personnel lockers and general storage, Building #4 was a stable converted to working space, and Building #5 was a vehicle maintenance shed. The large courtyard, more than 17,000 square feet, provided parking for battalion vehicles.

The availability of vernacular buildings and the needs of the National Guard created a serendipitous happenstance in St. Joseph that resulted in a Guard facility that served well for over thirty years. Designed by architect J. Kay Cleavinger and built in 1908 for Standard Oil, the main building and compound contained offices, vehicle parking, and storage areas. Standard Oil moved out of the compound in the early 1950s.

The compound offered the Guard drill space and storage in one location. The collection of buildings, taken together, formed a rectangular-shaped compound with a large, two-story brick office building facing south to Monterey Street, a long side with vehicular buildings fronting Ninth Street, and a garage fronting north on Sacramento Street. A large motor pool/parking area formed by the buildings on three sides faced a long alley to the west.[30] The National Guard moved into the Ninth and Monterey armory in 1955. The 135th Signal Battalion stayed there until a new armory was built in 1988 at Faraon and Woodbine Road in St. Joseph.

30. K. E. Jones, Standard Oil Property Real Estate Assessment, May 16, 1975, St. Joseph folder, MNGFE.

Fig. 2.52: Headquarters 146th Engineer Battalion Armory, ca. 1950

1701 East Eighteenth Street, Kansas City, Jackson County

Style: commercial vernacular

Built 1924; occupied by Guard ca. 1949–50

Architect/builder unknown

Photo: MMMH

This was the armory of the 242nd Engineer Battalion, the first Negro National Guard unit authorized in Missouri since the 1870s.

Fig. 2.53: Missouri National Guard Military Academy and Armory, 1997

1416 Monroe Street, Centertown, Cole County

Style: vernacular

Built 1924–1952; occupied by Guard 1984–present

Architect/builder: John M. Schaper, F. R. George

Photo: Chuck MacFall

In 1984, a schoolhouse in Cole County was converted into a National Guard Military Academy. The original building was constructed in 1924 and a second floor added by the WPA in the 1930s. A third addition to the rear was added in 1952. On April 12, 1984, the School District of Jefferson City sold the schoolhouse and surrounding grounds to the Missouri Guard.

Fig. 2.54: Brownfield Armory/former Battery D, 128th Field Artillery Armory, 2000
301 Sixth Street, Boonville, Cooper County
Style: German vernacular
Built 1927; occupied 1927–1939
Architect/builder: Cochran and Son
Photo: Chuck MacFall

After many years of moving from place to place, the Boonville National Guard finally landed a place to call home in 1927 when Earl Brownfield, a Boonville businessman, donated a lot worth $9,000 and built a building worth $16,000 on Sixth Street for a unit armory. The armory was built in 1927 by Cochran and Sons and was designed for use by both the local Guard unit and the community. The Boonville National Guard used this building from 1927 until 1939.[31] During those years, the building housed Battery "D" 128th Field Artillery and a medical detachment. Total personnel at the armory was seven officers and ninety-three enlisted men, and the Guard unit had an annual budget of $26,000 in federal and state funds. The building was large enough to house unit equipment, including trucks and cannon. The Guard unit remained here until 1939, when it moved to a new location with more space for vehicles and equipment.

According to the *Boonville Weekly Advertiser*, at the time it was built, the Brownfield Armory was the finest Guard building outside of St. Louis and Kansas City. During World War II, the armory was home to Company H and the medical department of the Fourth Missouri State Guard until the return of the regular National Guard units. The building was constructed entirely of brick and steel with a steel-truss roof; it contained a 20-by-20-foot office in the northeast corner, two 18-by-20-foot supply rooms, shower facilities, a 30-by-75-foot all-concrete drill hall, a dirt floor 60-by-75-foot vehicle storage area, and a 20-by-30-foot shop room.[32]

31. Reynolds, "History of the Development of a Permanent National Guard Armory in Boonville," 17.
32. "Earl Brownfield to Build Armory," *Boonville Weekly Advertiser*, May 13, 1927.

Fig. 2.55: Tatum Building/Battery E, 203rd Coast Artillery Armory, ca. 1950
101 Main Street, Anderson, McDonald County
Style: parapet commercial front
Built 1928; occupied by Guard 1927–1956
Architect/builder unknown
Photo: MMMH

Located on the main commercial street in Anderson, this building is a rusticated commercial storefront. At the center of the roof parapet is a rectangular stone plaque with the name of the builder and the date, "George Tatum 1928," inscribed on it.

The Anderson unit was federally organized in January 1922 as the Second Artillery, Missouri National Guard (anti-aircraft), but locally known as the "Houn' Dawg" regiment. Later it became part of the regionally famous 203rd Coast Artillery (AA). The Tatum Building became the armory for the 203rd beginning in 1927 when the unit moved from a room above the Barnes Appliance Store. The unit leadership selected the Tatum Building, with its large open floor space and storage area, as being suitable for large motor vehicles and associated artillery equipment.

In 1935 the unit commander, Captain Victor E. Tatum, was tasked by the Guard state headquarters to sound out the community about building a new armory under the WPA program. He sought advice from local community supporters, such as the Commercial Club in Anderson, and formed a committee to promote the new armory. At first the committee members thought they would be able to fund a new building or purchase a site, but they needed an additional $1,700. Although Tatum reported to headquarters that the community was "almost 100% for their unit of the National Guard," they could not raise the additional funds or find a suitable location. In his report, Tatum stated, "This unit has a suitable armory which is well located, and there will be no unfavorable reaction if the program is not carried out."[33]

The unit left for World War II from this building and was reactivated in 1946 in the same building. While the unit was absent during World War II, the armory was home to a company of temporary State Guards. In a 1950s photo, the central window bay transom holds a plaque in the shape of a hound dog, the symbol of the regiment. The 203rd, reorganized as Company A, 203rd Armor, moved into a new armory in 1956.[34]

33. Victor E. Tatum to Harold W. Brown, November 16, 1935, Anderson folder, MMMH.
34. Victor E. Tatum manuscript [personal remembrance], n.d., 10, Anderson folder, MMMH.

Fig. 2.56: Boonville Street Armory, ca. 1950
338 Boonville, Springfield, Greene County
Style: one-story modern
Built ca. 1930; occupied by Guard ca. 1950
Architect/builder unknown
Photo: MMMH

Fig. 2.57: North Jefferson Street Armory, ca. 1960
1630 North Jefferson, Springfield, Greene County
Style: one-story commercial
Built ca. 1930; occupied by Guard ca. 1960
Architect/builder unknown
Photo: MMMH

Fig. 2.58: Headquarters Company 140th Infantry Armory, 1939
Street address unknown, Marston, New Madrid County
Style: German vernacular
Built ca. 1938; occupied by Guard 1939–1958
Architect/builder unknown
Photo from *Historical Annual*, 1939

The town of Marston in southeastern Missouri housed a Guard unit and a school gym in a shared facility for many years. Marston gained a Guard unit possibly as early as 1927 when Headquarters Company of the First Battalion, 140th Infantry moved from Bertrand to Marston. The first Guard home in Marston was a wooden gymnasium building located on the grounds of the Marston Public School. The gym was two hundred feet from adjacent buildings and was used solely by the Guard unit and the school for physical education purposes. A 1928 inspection report noted the inadequacies of this building: a special concern was the fire potential in the wood structure even though the school mounted three 2 1/2-gallon fire extinguishers for emergency use. The report summarized the armory situation as "the best that the town affords."[35]

The subsequent armory building occupied by Headquarters Company was also a school gymnasium within sight of the old wood gym, built sometime in 1937 and 1938, but this time it was brick. The basement for the new red brick gymnasium was dug by volunteer help using mules and wagons. The majority of the building was devoted to the gym/drill hall floor with seating and stage space on either side of the floor. The basement area provided room for heating, locker room, and toilet facilities.

Headquarters Company moved into its new home in 1939, just in time to be federalized during President Roosevelt's prewar call up of the National Guard. The unit returned to the Marston armory in 1946 and stayed in its shared facility until moving to Portageville in 1958.

---

35. Willard P. Russell, "Annual Armory Inspection Report, April 20, 1928," Boonville Armory folder, MMMH.

Fig. 2.59: American Legion Hall/former Service Battery, 128th Field Artillery
Armory, 1998
625 East Morgan Street, Boonville, Cooper County
Style: vernacular box
Built 1948; occupied by Guard 1948–1978
Architect/builder: Stretz and Schuster
Photo: MMMH

The last privately built armory for the Boonville Guard was home to Battery D, Medical Detachment; Service Battery, 128th Field Artillery; the 1175th Military Police Battalion; and American Legion Thomas-Tuttle Post 52.

A space problem compelled the Boonville Guard to relocate again in 1948, just as the Cold War period forced the Guard to demand larger accommodations for more equipment. With only two weeks for the Guard to find new accommodations or face disbandment, the City of Boonville once again came to the rescue. This time the American Legion offered to build an armory for the Guard. The Legion provided $20,000 for the building, which was repaid in five years through Guard rents and other activities. The building was built in 1948 by Stretz and Schuster.[36]

For thirty-three years, the Guard remained the tenant in the Legion building. During this time the unit was reorganized several times. In 1978, during the Vietnam conflict, nationwide recruitment problems forced the Missouri Guard to find a cheaper building for the Boonville unit. Rather than disband, the unit chose to relocate.[37] The building is currently in commercial use.

36. L. Harper and J. Higbie. "Armory, October 1979," Historic Inventory Form, MO SHPO.

37. Reynolds, "History of the Development of a Permanent National Guard Armory in Boonville," 21.

Fig. 2.60: IOOF Hall/former Headquarters Company, 140th Infantry Armory, 1997
Old 67 Highway South, Farmington, St. Francois County
Style: step parapet vernacular
Built 1950; occupied by Guard ca. 1950
Architect: State Director of National Guard Facilities/Walter Smith
Photo: Chuck MacFall

Fig. 2.61: Romines Building/former Company C, 1138th Engineer Battalion Armory, 1997
115 Mill Street, Houston, Texas County
Style: commercial vernacular
Built ca. 1950; occupied by Guard 1991–1993
Architect/builder unknown
Photo: Wiegers

Fig. 2.62: Former Headquarters and Headquarters Detachment, 735th Maintenance Battalion Armory, 1997

2413 East McCarty Street, Jefferson City, Cole County

Style: modern vernacular

Built ca. 1950; occupied by Guard ca. 1983 (currently used by State Highway Patrol)

Architect/builder unknown

Photo: Wiegers

Fig. 2.63: Former Headquarters Detachment, 205th Medical Battalion Armory, 2002

502 & 506A East State Street, Mountain Grove, Wright County

Style: ranch

Built ca. 1960; occupied by Guard 1988–1996 (currently used by City of Mountain Grove)

Architect/builder unknown

Photo: MMMH

Fig. 2.64: 735th Ordnance Armory, ca. 1960
Buehler Park, Rolla, Phelps County
Style: cinder block box
Built ca. 1961, occupied by Guard ca. 1960s
Architect/builder unknown
Photo: MMMH

This utilitarian building is an example of common architecture the Missouri Guard has occupied from time to time. It is the opposite of some of the high-style architecture seen in other armories. It is unknown how long the detachment of the 735th stayed here or why it was assigned to this stand-alone building.

Fig. 2.65: 142nd Transportation Battalion Armory, ca. 1980
Highway 5 North, Lebanon, Laclede County
Style: commercial box
Built ca. 1970; occupied by Guard ca. 1980
Architect/builder unknown
Photo: MMMH

Fig. 2.66: Clasbey Community Center/Company B, 735th Support Battalion Armory, 1989

502 East Duncan Drive, Savannah, Andrew County

Style: vernacular box

Built ca. 1970; occupied by Guard 1989–1995

Architect/builder unknown

Photo: Chuck MacFall

During the time the Guard drilled at the community center, it utilized one half of the building and the community center the other half. When the Guard departed, their portion of the building reverted to the community center.

Fig. 2.67: Company D, 735th Support Battalion Armory, 1993

HCR 2, Eldon, Miller County

Style: commercial box

Built ca. 1977; occupied by Guard 1989–1995

Architect/builder unknown

Photo: Chuck MacFall

Fig. 2.68: Major John Hack Memorial Armory, 1998
900 Industrial Drive, Trenton, Grundy County
Style: commercial vernacular
Built 1985; occupied by Guard 1989–present
Architect/builder unknown
Photo: Chuck MacFall

The Guard armory in Trenton, Missouri, is a distinct vernacular building due to its original function and its basic construction. The armory is home to Company B, 135th Signal Battalion, Company B, 735th Main Support Battalion, and Organizational Maintenance Shop #16. It was originally designed and built as a truck terminal for the McCarty Trucking Company in 1985. When the trucking company went bankrupt, the land and building reverted to the City of Trenton. The Guard at the time was searching for a new armory in the area and entered into a deal with the city. The State of Missouri purchased the building and land for $205,000 in 1989. The City of Trenton donated an additional fourteen acres of land valued at $68,000.[38]

38. "Trenton Receives Federal Check for New National Guard Armory," *Chillicothe Constitution-Tribune*, December 21, 1989.

Chapter 3
Castle Armories
The Castellated Category

A building dedicated primarily to armory functions was a rarity prior to the mid-1800s.[1] In the latter half of the nineteenth century, more volunteer units sought to acquire a unit-owned armory to correct problems inherent in most rented spaces. Light Battery A in St. Louis determined to break away from the use of rental property by designing and constructing a unit-owned armory, already a trend in armory construction popular in eastern states. The building was completely financed by its own organization, the St. Louis Light Artillery Armory Association, which built the most elaborate "castle armory" in Missouri. The popularity of the castellated armory style, often referred to as medieval castle revival style, was an outgrowth of the movement to privately built armories. Although there are few of these in Missouri, castellated armories are the most noticeable architecturally, with crenellations, parapets, towers, and narrow windows.

The castellated style started on the East Coast and filtered westward, reaching Missouri prior to the start of the twentieth century. Although many castellated armories were built with private funds, some of the largest castellated armories in the eastern states were built with state funding or a combination of state and private funding. In Missouri, the castellated armories were built with local funding and state encouragement; hence they are scaled-down versions of the grandest armories in New York City, such as the White Plains Armory, the Seventh Regiment Armory, and the largest, the Kingsbridge Armory.[2]

Historically, St. Louis City accommodated most of Missouri's castellated armories. In 1899, the prestigious St. Louis Light Artillery Armory Association built a castellated armory with private funds; the building was used well into the 1960s (see fig. 3.2). In 1907, the First Infantry Regiment of Missouri built an armory in castellated style on Grand Avenue at Clark and Manchester Streets (see fig. 3.4). The last castellated armory built with private subscriptions was the 1909 armory in Nevada, Missouri. This armory clearly has many traits of a castle, such as towers and crenellations, but also has much in common with vernacular buildings of the era (see fig. 3.5). Other castellated armories built with state funding include the 110th Engineer Armory in Kansas City and the later WPA Pierce City armory. The popularity of the castellated style began to wane and in the years prior to World War I, it was gradually replaced by the modern style armory.

Many castellated armories, however, were still in use during the post–World War I era. In 1919,

1. Fogelson, *America's Armories*, 11.
2. Koch, "Medieval Castle Revival: New York Armories."

the chief of the US Militia Bureau, the highest-ranking National Guard officer in Washington DC, reported to the War Department that in many states, armories were owned by the state or municipality or by organizations of concerned citizens. The chief estimated the value of these armories at $36 million and considered them to be generally of better quality than armory buildings rented or leased by the state.

An interesting admonition accompanies the report on armories; the chief suggested that future armory designs include space for "amusement and club purposes and for adequate bathing facilities." The castellated armories, especially the larger examples, had these amenities, which was good for unit morale and promoted successful recruiting, an imperative with volunteer units.[3] Later styles continued to include clubrooms until the practice was discontinued in the Cold War era when after-hours socializing lost its importance in the life of the unit.

Gothic Revival and Castellated Armories

Gothic Revival architecture, using styles inspired by medieval castles and cathedral architecture, was part of the Romantic movement, which began in the eighteenth century and lasted until the mid-nineteenth century. Reacting to the Industrial Revolution and the Enlightenment, the Romantic movement emphasized emotion over reason and the senses over intellect, and revived an interest in folk culture, cultural origins, and the Middle Ages. In the wake of the physical and social destruction caused by the Napoleonic wars, architects and builders turned away from classical styles and to a romanticized vision of the age of chivalry, looking to Gothic art and architecture for inspiration. The spread of the Gothic revival style was aided by the popularity of Gothic novels that featured castles and other medieval trappings and literary figures who promoted the virtues and religiosity of the Middle Ages as a model for moral living. The Gothic revival style became the architectural embodiment of those ideals. The style was further popularized in the United States by the architectural plans of Alexander Jackson Davis and landscape designer Andrew Jackson Downing. In 1835, writer Washington Irving initiated a trend with his Gothic revival estate at Tarrytown, New York. His Sunnyside country house became the hallmark of Gothic revival in America. The style spread initially in ecclesiastical buildings, which include Richard Upjohn's Trinity Church in New York (completed in 1841) and Renwick's St. Patrick's Cathedral in New York (completed in 1859).

In the United States and England, the Gothic revival style remained popular after the Civil War and through the late nineteenth century and the early twentieth century as part of the Victorian style, a refinement of the Gothic revival style. Also called the High Victorian Gothic, this style was distinguished by perpendicularity, heavy decoration and stone carving, multicolored masonry, and Romanesque arches. Other common features included pointed or quatrefoil-shaped windows, often with delicate tracery and leaded glass, chimneys grouped in twos or threes, battlements and parapets, and the distinctive bay windows.

The largest concentration of Gothic revival castles is found along New York's Hudson River, nicknamed America's Rhine. During the colonial period, the Hudson River Valley was the home to many European-style manors, and even after the American Revolution, the descendents of the Dutch settlers living in that area persisted in considering themselves American aristocracy.[4] Many of these families built castles between 1870 and 1930 that reflect a strain of that pseudo-aristocratic

3. Militia Bureau, *Annual Report . . . 1919*, 3966–67.
4. Johnson, "Gallant Gothic."

heritage. Most castle owners in the Hudson Valley were self-made men of European descent and were aware of the historical association between the lord, his manor, and land. They wanted to convey in stone the qualities of strength, nobility, and power. Instead of doing this in a classical design, these American kings of industry followed popular culture into the medieval period, building in Gothic revival designs to proclaim their elite social status.[5]

Although the Gothic style is found throughout Europe, the Gothic revival styles—Norman, early English, decorated, and perpendicular—are found only in Great Britain and the United States. There are several reasons for the rise of Gothic revival in these places. First is the appearance of architectural books detailing medieval designs, giving a world accustomed to Palladian classicism an alternative style through realistic drawings of famous buildings. The second reason is that designers and builders promoted the Gothic revival as a culturally accepted style. The philosophical basis for the style was provided by designers August W. N. Pugin and John Ruskin, who connected the use of Gothic design elements to living a moral life and being a financial success. Nothing in this design philosophy hints at a military nature, rather it is a purely whimsical creation that glorifies the perceived best qualities of a past age. The most widely recognized Gothic revival buildings are the New Houses of Parliament (1836 to 1865) in London designed by Sir Charles Barry and A. W. N. Pugin, and the Bavarian Gothic revival castle Neuschwanstein. In America, variations of this style are found in the National Cathedral in Washington, DC.

The Gothic style promoted by Pugin had a tremendous impact on housing in America. The growing middle class adapted his designs to fit their individual circumstances. In contrast to the stone and brick cathedrals and castles in eastern states, the small Gothic revival house became a mainstay of Midwest architecture in the form of basic wood houses with peaked roofs and arched windows.[6] Reality was reflected in art when painter Grant Wood used a typical Gothic house he found in Eldon, Iowa, for the background in his famous painting *American Gothic*.

The popularity of the Gothic revival style had waned in Europe by the late nineteenth century, but in Britain and the United States, the Gothic style continued to be popular for churches and for academic and public buildings well into the twentieth century. Castellated armories are an enduring example of the continued popularity of the Gothic revival style in America.

There is little to connect the Gothic revival style with militia armories as a natural fit other than surface similarities: the Gothic revival style resembles a fortress and the armory houses the military arm of the state. However, turn-of-the-century social unrest provided a law enforcement mission for the militia that reinforced the connection between the two. The logical assumption, therefore, is that the militia and social unrest made it inevitable that new armories would be built like a castle so the militia could defend itself against a storming in a Bastille-like scenario.

Few can debate the high level of tension in American society in the later part of the nineteenth century. The working class felt controlled and exploited by the industrial giants of the day and anger sometimes led to violence. The middle class tended to sympathize more with the elite and therefore shared their fear of the possibility of violence from the working class, leading the middle class to react in a legal and traditional manner by supporting a citizen militia. The post–Civil War militia was reawakened in the late nineteenth century by the need for an extra-police force that was armed and trained to protect life and property. What is questionable is the assumption that Gothic revival

5. Bell, "Castles in America," 53, 57.

6. Aaltonen, *History of Architecture*, 180.

was the obvious style for new armory construction because this style held the greatest potential for militia protection.[7]

In some eastern cities, those with comparatively large numbers of immigrant workers, as well as in St. Louis and Kansas City, fear spurred the upper classes to support raising militia forces and to finance buildings to house them. In many cases, these buildings may have been intended to serve as a fortress, but it is just as likely that when considering architecture styles, the mental image of a castle came to mind as suited to repel a mob. If there was a natural reason to build a castle rather than a typical nineteenth-century fortification, the castle was the logical choice due to its smaller size. Most US coastal fortifications and forts are large in scale and contain many buildings. Clearly a real fortress on Main Street America was not feasible, but a castle could fit.

Common knowledge held that castles came in a variety of sizes and shapes and were encompassed by walls. Within the castle close, where the lord and his household were protected, the militia could be housed and protected. But the common vernacular or classical style building with modifications could have sufficed had it not been for the influence of popular American culture that had already accepted the Gothic revival style as an American norm. Culture had more to do with castellated armories than the fear-driven need for armory-fortresses.

One illustrated history of New York armory architecture focuses on the defensive features of the Gothic revival castellated style, devoting several pages to explanations of castle-like features useful in defending a fortress against mob violence, such as a sally port and portcullis.[8] The utility of these features is not in question as much as the selection of a Gothic revival-style armory building over a vernacular or classic style building that included those defensive features. The counterargument is that the style was selected by a number of militias less because of its defensive capabilities than because it was in fashion at the time and therefore the logical choice.

With all the military attributes of the castle so evident, it is worth noting two important considerations that counter the apparent positives. First, a true castle has layered defenses, so an attacker who breaks into one defensive ring is simply confronted with another. The American armories built in Gothic revival castellated style may have parts of an outer ring of defense, but on the inside, the armory is more home than fortress, with easily reached rooms, halls, and stairs. The second and major factor against the argument that the style was chosen for its defensive features is that the militia needed to be in the city during mob violence; if the militia were safe within its keep, they would not be on the streets confronting the rapacious mob. Other building styles could have served the militia as a secure home base in troubled times; in fact, any building constructed with defense in mind would have served as well. The Gothic castle just happened to be the current style, and in that respect, the obvious choice for an armory.

Other reasons account for the preponderance of castle-like armories built in the late nineteenth to early twentieth centuries. The most telling is wealth and social standing of militia leaders, who were often successful men in the community. As with private castle-style residences, militia leaders viewed their building as a reflection of their own status. The volunteer militia felt they were a cut above the ordinary militia; having a castellated armory proved a unit was a step above other volunteer units that were still housed in vernacular buildings.

7. Fogelson, *America's Armories,* xv.
8. Todd, *New York's Historic Armories,* 4–7.

The Gothic revival or castellated armories are the first armories built in a uniform architectural style in many states. In longstanding tradition, many of these armories are the product of unit efforts to build their own homes rather than continuing to rent inadequate facilities. As functional buildings for the Guard, the castellated armories served as well as any other style. Functionality aside, these often-ornate buildings are a superb reflection of the Guard's martial image, which have been matched but not surpassed by later styles.

The castellated armory style never achieved celebrity status in Missouri equal to its popularity in the East as reflected by the number of castellated armories built in some eastern states. Today there are few extant specimens of these armories in Missouri, as demolition has winnowed their number. Whether the style was popular for its military value or for show, the result was a building that was impressive to the viewer and a reflection of the militia function inside. Both the style and the social message appealed to the middle- and upper-class citizens of major US cities in the later nineteenth century.

Inventory of Castellated Armories (by date built)

Fig. 3.1: Missouri State Armory-Arsenal, ca. 1900
Broadway and Stewart Streets, Jefferson City, Cole County
Style: castellated
Built ca. 1863; occupied ca. 1863–ca. 1909
Architect/builder unknown
Photo: MMMH

Although this building was constructed as a state arsenal (i.e., for arms storage) in 1863, it was also used as a National Guard State Headquarters and armory during certain years. This building represents the only armory built by the state in support of the Missouri Militia in the pre– and post–Civil War periods. Although the facility was built in 1863, by 1869 the adjutant general was already calling for repairs to the structure due to a leaking roof.[9] Finally in 1897/98, the building was remodeled, and according to Adjutant General Bell, the new offices were "an index to the progressiveness of a great state."[10] From this location, the adjutant general directed the resurrection of the state militia from the chaos of the Civil War until it was demolished around 1910.

The first floor at one time became an armory for a local Guard unit, and also held offices for the state geologist. The adjutant general apparently controlled most of the second floor. This building not only held the offices of the adjutant general of Missouri and his staff, but at times it also held all state weaponry and equipment either state-purchased or transferred from the federal government, and a small museum and archive.[11]

9. Adjutant General, *Annual Report . . . 1869*, 9.

10. Adjutant General, *Report . . . 1897–1898*, 6.

11. Ibid.

Fig. 3.2a (above): Architectural drawing of proposed armory in St. Louis, from *St. Louis Republic*, 1898.

Fig. 3.2: St. Louis Light Artillery Armory Association Armory, 1909
1221 South Grand Avenue, St. Louis
Style: castellated
Built 1899; occupied 1899–ca. 1940
Architect/builder: Louis C. and William M. Bulkley
Photo from *Biennial Report of the Adjutant General 1909–1910*

The St. Louis Light Artillery Armory Association building on South Grand Avenue in St. Louis was built in 1899, an example of private citizens supporting the National Guard by providing an unmistakable castle-like home. The influence of the Richardsonian Romanesque style, a variation of Gothic revival and Victorian named for its originator, Boston architect H. H. Richardson (1838–86), can be seen in the detailing of the grand half-round entrance archway centered in the long stretch of blank wall with bands of windows, and the round towers embedded in the wall. The building is rectangular-shaped with a flat roof and constructed of gray brick masonry with stone and terra cotta ornamentation.

In 1897, Missouri Guard's local St. Louis unit's Captain Frank M. Rumbold, a medical doctor, inventor, veteran of the Spanish-American War and Philippine Insurrection, and future adjutant general of the Missouri Guard, reported to the then-adjutant general that St. Louis Light Artillery Armory Association had purchased a lot on the highest point in the city for $10,000. Located on South Grand Avenue between Hickory and Rutger, the lot measured 190 feet 8 inches by 218 feet 3 inches and was west of the city, close to Civil War–era Fort Fremont. At the time, this area was relatively undeveloped, but was a natural avenue for westward expansion from the city core. The lot was also conveniently close to the Mill Creek Valley railroads. The Guard unit had the lot fenced and members of the battery unit graded the lot themselves and laid two hundred loads of cinders over it to create an all-weather surface. Tents were used for temporary office space and the unit built a twenty-by-seventy-five-foot barracks for storage.[12]

Funding for construction of the armory building came from the sale of St. Louis Light Artillery Armory Association stock in 1899. This civic organization, founded in 1830 to promote militia and National Guard interests in the city, sold stock for fifty dollars a share. Association president A. L. Shapleigh promoted the purchase of stock as more of a donation to a civic enterprise than an investment; however, the association was able to pay a dividend of 50 percent to stockholders in June 1941 and again in 1943.[13] A listing of stockholders from those years shows that most were from the middle class and above, including many individuals and corporations that were well-known in the early 1900s and still resonate today: Brown Shoe Company, Mallenckrodt Chemical Co., Scruggs-Vandervoort-Barney, the Terminal Railroad Association, Adolphus Busch III, the *St. Louis Globe-Democrat*, Anheuser-Busch Brewing Co., Frank M. Rumbold, Louis Lemp, May Department Stores, Manufacturers Bank and Trust Co., and many more.[14] In true volunteer fashion, by 1899, the Association had acquired enough money from gifts, fundraisers, and stock interest to build the four-story structure facing Grand Avenue. The overall plan was to complete the main armory on Grand Avenue and then start collecting funds to enclose the whole block into an armory square. Unfortunately, construction of the second phase never occurred because planning for the Louisiana Purchase Exposition in 1904 made fundraising more difficult.[15] The association maintained the property and survived well into the next century when the federal government began funding the construction of armories on a large scale, making privately owned armories a rarity.

The armory was designed to be fireproof. Little wood was used in the interior; only the roof of the drill hall, which was built on steel trusses, and the finish trim in the rooms were made of wood. All floors were constructed of steel beams and concrete.[16] Unlike most armories in Missouri, the designers of this armory, Louis C. and William M. Bulkley, envisioned the armory as a bastion of defense against a mob—understandable in St. Louis where memories of the 1870s riots spurred the formation of many city militia units.

The finished armory was 190 feet long, 30 feet wide, and three stories high. A planned one-story drill hall of 179 feet by 182 feet to be located at the rear of the lot was never built. The armory's roof was carried by six trusses leading to a height of 60 feet in the center. The first floor contained the "stable" area for guns and ambulances, the quartermaster's storeroom, workshops for artificers, and the harness room. Located in the center of the building facing Grand Avenue was the only entrance, 16 feet wide to accommodate caissons and gun carriages. To the right of the entry was an "imposing stairway" (in the words of a *St. Louis Republic* reporter) leading to the floors above. The second floor held the company parlor, officers' quarters, lavatories, hospital corps, and quartermaster's room. The third floor held the company locker room, lavatories, and baths. The two towers were not merely decorative: the south tower held the armorers' quarters and the north tower held the magazines and storeroom. The boiler room was on the first floor below the harness room.[17] Inside the fenced compound was a spacious outdoor drill yard with a full-length second-floor observation platform overlooking the drill yard from the rear of the main building.

12. Adjutant General, *Report . . . 1897–1898*, 78–79.

13. "Battery 'A' Repaying Stockholders in Full After 44 Years," *St. Louis Globe-Democrat*, March 28, 1943.

14. Lists of stockholders from St. Louis Light Artillery Association Papers, 1941–1943, Light Artillery Association folder, MMMH.

15. "Battery 'A' Armory," *St. Louis Post-Dispatch*, May 17, 1940.

16. "Light Battery 'A' Will Have a New Home on Grand Avenue," *St. Louis Republic*, April 15, 1893.

17. Ibid.

As a privately supported militia unit, Battery A depended on two elements in St. Louis society for existence. The unit needed the backing of the commercial interests in the town and the participatory interest of a small segment of the population for recruits. An armory with amenities and a martial-look facilitated that end.

The St. Louis Light Artillery Armory Association was almost dissolved on May 16, 1956, when its assets, including the Battery A Armory, were turned over to the city. At the time the Association had $12,236 in cash, government bonds worth $84,000, and the armory on South Grand Avenue, which was assessed at $110,000; the value of the whole city block was estimated at $250,000.[18] After turning its assets over to the city, the Association retained only its corporate charter. Battery A was moved to the 138th Infantry Armory on Market Street in 1946.

At one time, the Missouri National Guard had been interested in acquiring the South Grand Avenue property and renovating it to serve as a city armory. Unfortunately for the armory, state law barred the Missouri Guard from improving a property if it did not hold the title.[19] Conflicting interests between the Association, the city, and the Guard prevented a quick transfer of title from the city to the Guard, and the site was left to the city for disposal. On September 4, 1958, St. Louis University bought the Battery A Armory and drill field for $100,000. Demolition of the sixty-two-year-old building began in mid-July 1960, and in two weeks it was gone. The lot became the site of the university's David P. Wohl Health Institute.[20]

Fig. 3.3: Company D, 1138th Engineer Battalion Armory, 1997

Highway 63, Macon, Macon County

Style: castellated

Built 1900; occupied by Guard 1986–2001

Architect/builder: R. G. Kirsch and Co.

Photo: Chuck MacFall

18. "City Receives Assets," *St. Louis Post-Dispatch*, May 16, 1956.
19. "Legal Red Tape Bars Disposal of Armory Here," *St. Louis Globe-Democrat*, December 31, 1954.
20. "Battery A Turrets Falling Before Wreckers' Onslaught," *St. Louis Globe-Democrat*, July 13, 1960.

In the tradition of rented armories, the facility on Highway 63 in Macon was not built to be an armory. The Blees Military Academy Gymnasium was built in 1900 as part of a school campus. When it was completed, the gymnasium building, designed by architect R. G. Kirsch and Co., was reported to be the most modern gymnasium west of the Mississippi River. It had an indoor swimming pool on the first floor and a one-twelfth-mile track running around the inside on an elevated balcony. Also on the ground floor were rooms for gym equipment, a target range, a bowling alley, shower rooms, and lockers.[21]

Prior to 1900, the school had been St. James Academy. It was converted into a military academy under the leadership of Colonel Frederick Wilhelm Blees, who was born in 1860 in Aachen and served in the Prussian army before immigrating to the United States. After teaching in a number of states, Blees became superintendent of St. James Academy in 1890. In 1900, he converted the school into a 143-acre military academy and changed its name to the Blees Military Academy. After Colonel Blees died in St. Louis in 1906, the academy soon went bankrupt and closed. The buildings remained vacant for several years, then the property was sold and became the Still-Hildreth Osteopathic Sanitarium in 1914.[22] The gymnasium building was greatly altered; large areas were divided into smaller rooms and the pool may have been filled in. The sanitarium occupied the premises until 1968.[23] Between 1972 and 1984, the property was owned by the City of Macon and remained vacant. In 1984, the main building became a low-income housing facility, and in 1986, the Missouri National Guard occupied the gymnasium building, using it as an armory until the unit moved into a new armory in 2001. In 2007, the City of Macon entered into an agreement with the Macon County Historical Society allowing the society to use the Blees Annex Building, which now houses the Macon County Museum.

Fig. 3.4: First Regiment Armory, 1938
Grand Avenue at Market Street, St. Louis City
Style: castellated
Built 1907; occupied 1907–1938
Architect/builder unknown
Photo: WHMC-STL

This turn-of-the-century castellated armory belonged to the St. Louis First Regiment, National Guard of Missouri. The First Regiment had been quartered in a smaller facility on Seventeenth and Pine Streets in 1895. The Regimental Association had a building worth $60,000 at the site, but lost the right to own

21. "New Blees Military Academy Gymnasium," *Macon Citizen*, January 11, 1901.

22. "The Still Sanitarium Is Coming to Macon," *Macon Chronicle-Herald*, September 4, 1913.

23. Irma Miller, "Col. Frederick Wilhelm Blees Built Academy Which Became Macon's Sanatorium," *Macon Chronicle-Herald*, August 3, 1974.

the land, putting its armory in jeopardy. The regiment made a deal exchanging the building for a lease, and managed to stay on that site until January 1, 1896, but the association needed to find a new home or disband the six-hundred-man regiment. While searching for a larger drill area, the Regimental Association learned that a group in St. Louis was searching for a suitably large auditorium for the Republican National Convention. The Republican Party subcommittee considered converting the north half of the existing Exposition Center into an auditorium, but the space was thought to be too small. An alternative was to build a temporary "wigwam" structure for the convention, but the cost was estimated at between $30,000 and $50,000—much too expensive for a temporary structure.

In one of those rare cases when the needs of the militia and state politicians almost blended together, the Guard unit and the subcommittee made a marriage of convenience.[24] The two groups decided to use the $30,000 to $50,000 estimated for a temporary structure as a starting point around which to raise funds for a permanent building. The goal was to have the auditorium and necessary facilities completed in time for the convention. That deadline proved to be impossible, but the plan to build the armory received the full support of the St. Louis Business Men's League and eventually became a reality.[25]

The two-story, rectangular-shaped armory was constructed of wood frame covered with stucco, with a flat roof behind a low, flat parapet. Centered in the parapet wall was a bas-relief carving of the seal of the State of Missouri. The building extended for 284 feet along Grand Avenue and 182 feet along Manchester and Clark Avenues. The frontage was recessed seventy feet from Grand Avenue for aesthetic purposes, and the rear abutted an alley. The interior arrangement allowed for forty-three rooms and a 100-by-200-foot drill hall. Other facilities included a forty-by-thirty-foot Officers Club, a twenty-five-by-thirty-foot quartermaster room, twelve company rooms of ten by forty feet each, and fourteen locker rooms for arms and equipment. The band, the colonel, and the staff each had separate rooms. Space was also provided for the engineering corps, the hospital corps, and noncommissioned officers.

Completed in January 1908, the armory cost about $100,000 ($60,000 for the lot and $40,000 for construction). Since the armory was built with private funds, the State of Missouri paid rent for use of the building. In February 1939, thirty-one years after the building was constructed, the First Regiment left the Grand Avenue armory for new quarters on Market Street, closer to downtown St. Louis. The fate of the old armory confirmed the temporary nature of the structure, even though it had been in use for thirty years. Several offers were made to buy the building from the First Regiment Armory Association for reuse as a hall or business establishment, but according to the St. Louis building commissioner, the armory had been issued only a temporary occupancy permit due to its frame construction. The temporary permit had been renewed periodically, but the change of tenants would require a new occupancy permit, which could not be issued because of the construction methods used. The building was razed in 1939.[26]

24. "For a New Armory," *St. Louis Post-Dispatch*, January 25, 1896.

25. "The Coming Court-Martial," *St. Louis Globe-Democrat*, February 4, 1896.

26. "Denied Permit," *St. Louis Post-Dispatch*, November 24, 1938.

Fig. 3.5: Company H, Second Infantry Armory, 1909
402 East Cherry Street, Nevada, Vernon County
Style: castellated
Built 1909; occupied 1909–1922
Architect: T. W. Blast / Builder: Daly Brothers Construction Co.
Photo from *Biennial Report of the Adjutant General 1909–1910*

The armory in Nevada is the last castellated armory built by a Guard unit in Missouri. The building was designed by T. W. Blast of Sedalia, Missouri, and built by the Daly Brothers Construction Co. in 1909. It was completed at a cost of $16,000, using funds raised by private subscription and unit fundraising. The Guard unit of Nevada, Missouri, may have paid for its building in the same way the Company B, Second Infantry unit of Holton, Kansas, paid for its building. Company B took the $300 per year they received from the state to rent an armory and the funds the unit received for each drill the men participated in and placed this money in the building fund, deferring other purchases until they repaid the construction loans.[27]

Much of the interior retains its original configuration. Both the towered north and south ends have office space with original tin ceilings. The drill hall covers the first floor, overlooked by a balcony that extends out from the offices at the south end of the building. When the unit moved in 1922, probably to an armory at nearby Camp Clark, the building became an American Legion Hall.[28]

27. Rafter, "Armory Experience of a Kansas Company."
28. Ref. no. H-13, 14, 402 East Cherry Street, Architectural/Historic Inventory Survey Form, October 1991, MO SHPO.

Fig. 3.6: 110th Engineer Battalion Armory, ca. 1950
3620 Main Street, Kansas City, Jackson County
Style: castellated
Built 1923; occupied 1923–1973
Architect/builder: General Stayton
Photo: MMMH

The 110th Engineer Armory was privately built and designed with castle-like elements. From the time it was being designed, the building was meant to be a focal point for all the local Guard units in Kansas City. Designed by General Stayton to be an armory serving many units, it was built in 1923 at a cost of $150,000.

This large building was home for many years to the 110th Engineer Combat Battalion. With two floors, the building had a capacity to house four hundred men or the equivalent of a regiment. The building held offices for headquarters and supply, company offices, locker rooms, a lounge, and a 90-by-160-foot drill hall. The basement housed the engineers, a shower-bath area, and a rifle range. Drill nights were dispersed throughout the week. Monday nights were reserved for headquarters and supply, Wednesdays were reserved for the First Battalion, and the Second Battalion used the building on Thursdays.[29]

Since the 110th Engineers departed for the New Ozark Road armory, the old armory has been converted to retail space.

29. "110th Engineers," *Kansas City Star*, September 8, 1922.

Fig. 3.7: Pierce City Armory, 1997

104 West Main Street, Pierce City, Lawrence County

Style: castellated

Built 1939; addition built 1958; occupied 1939–2003

Architect/builder: George Draper

Photo: Chuck MacFall

The Pierce City Armory was built in 1939 as a WPA project, but the design combines features of castellated architecture with the art deco/WPA style and the use of reinforced cement. This building reflects two architectural styles and could have been placed in the art deco/WPA category of this inventory, but it was categorized as castellated because of the prominent crenellations at the corners. Architect George Draper of Neosho may have intended to evoke the image of the castle by adding castellated elements at minimal expense to the otherwise art deco structure. Since the planned auditorium portion of the building was not built at the time, it is not possible to know how the complete building was intended to look. When the auditorium portion was built in 1958, it was constructed as a plain gym floor with a simple vaulted roof.

The building has two levels with the office wing tucked into the front section of the building. Entry for vehicles is through a single garage bay on the façade, where access slants downward from street level. The main entry to the building is a single doorway with access from the street up a narrow parapeted stone stair in two runs with a landing. Attached to the right long wall of the original WPA building is the 1958 addition with arched roofline facing the street (not seen in the photo). The original building is cement covered by a very light-colored Carthage stone.

The cost of the original armory building was underestimated, so the administrative portion of the armory was completed without the auditorium portion.[30] Some of the budget problems were due to material shortages, site flooding, and architectural adjustments. According to design specifications, materials used in construction of the armory included 55 tons of steel, "634 cubic yards of building stone, 584 cubic yards of chat, 550 tons of sand, 15,000 board feet of lumber, 4,000 bags of cement, 15,000 square feet of rock lath, 8,000 feet of insulation board, 24 tons of plaster, 80 rolls of roofing, and 2,800 pounds of asphalt."[31]

The completed armory had a vehicle storage area, a heating room, and a small-arms range in the lower level, and quartermaster stores, offices, locker rooms, and showers on the upper floors. Several upper-story rooms had doorways opening to the auditorium that was never built. In the postwar period, the issue of the state completing the armory became a sore spot with the Missouri Guard adjutant general. Pierce City had donated the land for an armory and community center, and was left with only half

30. A. D. Sheppard to Max Myers, April 14, 1953, Armory correspondence files, MMMH.

31. "Armory Requires Much Material," *Pierce City Leader-Journal*, July 18, 1940.

of the planned facility. At that point, the WPA no longer existed and there appeared to be little interest in completing the project, but the state's obligation to Pierce City weighed heavily on the adjutant general.[32] In 1953, a project to build the drill hall was brought up for extra funding and $137,500 was eventually budgeted. The arched drill hall designed by J. Carl Jourdan was attached in 1958. The new addition was destroyed by a tornado in 2003, but the original WPA building sustained only minor damage, losing its roof and some stone from the upper walls. The building has been repaired and remodeled, and is currently used by the city for office space and as a civic center.

---

32. A. D. Sheppard to Max Myers, April 14, 1953, Armory correspondence files, MMMH.

Chapter 4
Depression-Era Armories
The Art Deco/WPA Category

T he final report of the WPA, issued in 1946, noted that "A special feature of the [WPA's] building-construction program was the armory construction work carried out on a nation-wide scale. It was found that in many localities a building could combine all the features of an armory with those of a community meeting place or recreation center; and a combination armory and community center was very widely adopted in local plans. More than four hundred of these buildings were constructed, varying in cost from a few thousand to several hundred thousand dollars."[1] Many of these armories were built in a particular variant of the modern style called art deco. The modern style appeared in the late nineteenth century, flourished in the interwar years as art deco and was modified in the post–World War II years as another variation of the modern style. The modern movement emphasized a rejection of traditional and classical revival forms in art, architecture, literature, religion, and social organization, embracing science and technology as tools of progress and affirming the human ability to create and improve the built environment.

As it is reflected in architecture, the modern movement has had a lasting effect on the American built environment in a number of variations on the modern style. Architects and designers used modernist theories of simplicity and utility and the dictum of "form follows function" to develop the first skyscraper (St. Louis's Wainwright Building) to provide maximum space within a small plot of land, to create buildings that follow the natural lines of the existing environment (perhaps the most famous example is Frank Lloyd Wright's Fallingwater), and to abandon ornate ornamentation in favor of simpler designs that functioned to identify a building, signal its purpose, or emphasize its scale and lines.

The first modernist architectural and interior design style was art nouveau, which rejected the eclectic revival styles of the nineteenth century and emphasized stylized organic forms and sweeping curves inspired by the Beaux Arts style and details of the Arts and Crafts movement. World War I spurred the spread of the modern style by sweeping away the old ruling order, the old class society, and the old symbolism, but also swept away the art nouveau style in favor of a variant, art deco.[2] Art deco in turn was modified in the 1930s into the streamline moderne style, which paved the way for modern architecture in the postwar period. Although art deco and streamline moderne are part of the "modern movement," they are not the quintessential "modern" as used in the next chapter of this

---

1. Field, *Final Report on the WPA Program, 1935–1943,* 52.
2. Jencks, *What is Post-Modernism?*, 24–25.

volume. To avoid confusing labels, the WPA name is applied to this category because all armories in this group were funded by the Works Progress Administration and were built following WPA-approved plans. Not all WPA armories were built in art deco or streamline moderne style; some WPA armories were not included in this category because they primarily used vernacular building materials or other stylistic features.

In the post–World War I period, theatres, offices, and a large number of government buildings were built in art deco and streamline modern styles due to the entry of the US government in relief programs and other back-to-work programs. These buildings are easily identified by their use of distinctive decorations such as color, geometric forms like zigzags and sunbursts, and materials such as cement, metal, and glass. But for all their allure, the art deco style had limited popularity between World Wars I and II. The style continued to be used into the Depression years, when many building projects fell under the auspices of the WPA and the Public Works Administration (PWA), which funded the construction of many civic buildings. These agencies built so many courthouses, schools, bridges, dams, offices, and armories using agency-approved designs that a separate style was coined for them—PWA Moderne.[3]

The art deco style originated in 1925 at a Paris exposition dedicated to any design that disregarded the traditional. It has been described as a frame of mind as well as a building style, a modern but not modernist style, expressed in many ways by architects such as Frank Walker, Raymond Hood, and William Van Alen. Art deco influences are also seen in home and office décor, clothing and jewelry fashion, and mass-produced consumer products.[4] Art historian Ghislaine Wood described the art deco style as reflecting "an age of extremes, spanning the boom of the roaring twenties and the bust of the Depression-ridden thirties." The art deco style was certainly international, seen in the design of skyscrapers, office buildings, and industrial buildings around the world. But the art deco style was also amenable to nationalistic influences and was recognizable even when adapted to local forms and materials. When it originated in the 1920s, art deco expressed wealth and sophistication, emphasizing handcrafted elements that used simple geometric shapes and expensive materials. During the Depression, the style shifted to emphasizing the use of materials that could be mass-produced easily and cheaply, such as concrete, glass, and iron.[5]

The art deco style permeated all aspects of American culture more thoroughly than architectural movements typically did in part because modernism entered American culture first in one art style, then moved to another, then another. The art deco style developed at a time of postwar prosperity and in reaction to the forced austerity of wartime and the Depression, and at the same time, technological developments, mass production, and mass marketing aided the spread of art deco to a wider range of products and made those latest styles available to a new level of consumers. A simultaneous rise in the popularity of movies led to a dramatic increase in the construction of movie theaters, which in the early days were owned by the movie studios, who competed to build the most lavish theaters. In addition, movie studios embraced the art deco style in films as a popular symbol of wealth and sophistication. By the mid-1930s, over 80 million Americans per week attended the new movie houses, where they absorbed art deco styling as the height of modernity and a mark of financial success.[6]

3. Gebhard, *National Trust Guide to Art Deco in America*, 7.

4. Benton, Benton, and Wood, *Art Deco 1910–1939*, 13.

5. Wood, *Essential Art Deco*, 1–14.

6. Duncan, *American Art Deco*, 13–15; Benton, Benton, and Wood, *Art Deco 1910–1939*, 325–33.

One of the hallmarks of art deco was its eclecticism, and the classic example of its malleability was its incorporation of Egyptian-inspired motifs after the 1923 discovery of the tomb of Egyptian pharaoh Tutankhamun. Americans could not get enough of the details, and art deco artisans and architects could not find enough ways to incorporate Egyptian motifs, such as palm leaves, papyrus reeds, lotus flowers, and ankhs, into everyday products, such as telephones, picture frames, clothing and jewelry, wall treatments, and decorative reliefs. "Tutmania" had arrived and middle-class Americans could not escape it.[7]

As an ornamental style, art deco has been described as "just as flamboyant, but somehow more sassy" than art nouveau.[8] Art deco is visually bold with emphasis on the vertical plane. Architectural decoration consists of incised geometric patterns, especially chevrons and zigzags (i.e., a series of short sharp turns), and especially concentrated around the entrance, whereas art nouveau is more concerned with floral designs on the interior and exterior. One of the identifying marks of an art deco building is poured concrete, a radical new use for an old medium (see figs. 4.5, 4.8, 4.12, 4.15, 4.16, 4.17, 4.18, 4.23). Streamline moderne (a designation first used in 1969), which developed in the 1930s, was a continuation of the art deco tradition, but where art deco buildings emphasized vertical lines, the streamline moderne style emphasized the horizontal. The main elevation of a streamline moderne building is always flat with any vertical features grouped around the entrance. A second characteristic is curved end walls with wrap-around windows. Decoration such as incising is limited to stringcourses and trim (see figs. 4.21 and 4.22).[9] WPA modern is an interesting mix of old and new and is hard to define. In the context of armory architecture, WPA modern is art deco and streamline moderne combined, but built of local materials and evocative of patriotism and the past (see figs. 4.3, 4.4, 4.6, 4.7, 4.9, 4.10, 4.11, 4.13, 4.14, 4.19, 4.20, 4.24).

Decoration on Missouri's art deco armories is not as elaborate as that found on many commercial buildings, the result of the shortage of skilled workmen in many regions of Missouri during the Depression. Generally, Missouri armories have a smoothed concrete wall surface that is painted in neutral colors to allow the sun to pick up texture in the concrete. The famous low-relief incised geometric designs found in art deco are grouped around the entrance with little decoration elsewhere. The verticality that distinguishes art deco from other modern styles is illustrated in the Aurora (fig. 4.17) and Kirksville (fig. 4.18) armories.[10]

Two construction techniques are almost diagnostic of art deco, streamline moderne, and PWA/WPA modern armory buildings: the use of concrete and the lamellar roof. The innovation that made concrete so attractive in 1920 was the addition of shape-forming steel rods imbedded into the concrete to create ferroconcrete, that is, reinforced or monolithic concrete (poured in place as a single piece).[11] In building terms, this meant the architect could use ferroconcrete as he would use stone, wood, and iron to create a variety of shapes but without visible seams, and without the dangers of fire associated with wood or of slow decay or rust associated with iron or steel. The architectural versatility in ferroconcrete was limited only by the imagination, since it could be thickened with an aggregate and poured over the reinforcing rods to create a strong wall or thinned to create delicate tracery. Columbia

7. Benton, Benton, and Wood, *Art Deco 1910–1939*, 41–48.

8. Aaltonen, *History of Architecture*, 208.

9. Whiffen, *American Architecture since 1780*, 241.

10. Patterson, "Midwest Modern," 6.

11. Onderdonk, *Ferro-Concrete Style*, 3.

Fig. 4.1: Lamellar roof over the Columbia Armory, ca. 1939 (Photo: Dave Clark)

architect Dave Clark personally plunged his hands into the newly poured cement at the corner of the Columbia armory to ensure that the material was pushed into every leg and angle of each letter of the cornerstone. This way he was certain the cornerstone dedication would be crisp and clean when the mold was removed.[12] Surface texture could also be created by roughing the cement face to fit a design theme or to allow light and shadow to play on the surface to emphasize texture.[13]

In most WPA/art deco armories, the roofline was a combination of a flat roof over office areas and a vaulted roof over the drill hall floor. The construction technique for the vaulted roof section was the most unusual innovation in the WPA armories since it was free standing and constructed in a graceful arch composed of hundreds of short individual wood elements called lamellae. These were cut to exact specifications to be interlocked or "woven" into a honeycomb lattice that supported the external roofing material. The benefit of this technique was "in the easy handling and assembling of the similar, mass-produced components, which [was] accomplished by a simple hand-and-tool technique such as bolting."[14]

Developed in Germany and patented in the United States in 1925, the lamellar ceiling, or diagrid system of vault framing, is an architectural marvel. A St. Louis firm, the Missouri Lamella Roof Company, became the regional licensee for this new type of roofing system. The licensee and president of the Missouri Lamella Roof Company was Edward A. Faust, son-in-law of Adolphus Busch. The St. Louis Arena, which was built in 1929 near Forest Park and seated over 21,000 people,[15] had the largest lamellar roof in Missouri until it was razed on February 27, 1999.

The wide distribution of armories constructed in state-of-the-art styles across the United States is a result of the concurrence of the Depression and the Guard's need for new facilities. Up until the 1930s, most states were content to house their militia in vernacular buildings or ornate castellated-style armories, but the Spanish-American War initiated changes in the National Guard that by

12. Dave Clark to Robert Wiegers, personal communication, June 1991.

13. Ibid.

14. Condit, *American Building Art*, 40.

15. "Landmarks Letter."

Fig. 4.2: Lamellar ceiling, Doniphan Armory, ca. 1995 (Photo: Chuck MacFall)

1930 necessitated more and larger armories. Congressional attention to the Guard and US Army demands on the Guard drew increasing attention to the poor state of the nation's armories. By law, Guard armories were a state responsibility, and up until that point, the federal government had been content to overlook state neglect of militia housing needs. As the Depression deepened, the army and state adjutants general increasingly pressed for federal support of Guard units and better armories, yet Congress was not convinced of the need. Congressional opinion held if the states had been lax in providing adequate armory buildings, then it was a state problem.

The hard times of the Depression provided a solution to the impasse in Congress. As individual states became unable to care for the unemployed, the federal government, anxious to avert possible civil strife, stepped in with a variety of programs and Congress was finally convinced to unite the Guard's need for housing with the states' need for work relief, and unleash the power of the US Treasury. In 1930, the outlook for better federal funding was not good.[16] It was completely against precedent to have the federal government so intimately involved in state militia affairs, but hard times dictated that unusual steps must be taken. First, however, two groups had to come together to make it all happen.

The government program most responsible for the flurry of armory construction in the 1930s was the WPA.[17] The WPA was initiated in 1935, a successor to the Civil Works Administration and Federal Emergency Relief Administration, and generally concentrated on service and construction projects to put people on relief back to work. The WPA service projects sought to employ women and professionals in work ranging from community and civic projects, like the American Guide Series (which included *Missouri: The WPA Guide to the "Show Me" State*), to scientific research such as archaeological expeditions. The WPA construction work was most beneficial because it required the use of local labor and materials, providing economic stimulus from the bottom up, whereas the PWA funded construction projects in the traditional manner by letting contracts without labor and material requirements, providing economic stimulus from the top down. By June 1935, a $6 million

16. Militia Bureau, *Annual Report ... 1930*, 2.
17. Field, *Final Report on the WPA Program, 1935–1943*, iii.

national construction program for armories and other facilities had been submitted to the WPA. Although most of these projects were not immediately approved, the planning process allowed the WPA to draw up proposed floor plans, often based on submitted plans of local origin, and offer advice.[18]

How successful the WPA legislation and various construction programs were at creating jobs throughout the 1930s can be gauged by the number of those employed—WPA projects employed 75 percent of the WPA field workforce—and in the nine hundred armories built nationwide, of which over four hundred were a combination of armory and community center.[19] Yet armory construction accounted for less than one percent of all public buildings constructed under the WPA.[20] Although the government wanted to get Americans back to work, the money from Washington was not free; it required local matching funds. Municipalities that sought to capture funding for an armory project needed local political support, and had to complete the appropriate forms, locate a source of matching money, and compete with other towns for authorization.

Not all in Congress wanted National Guard projects to be included in the Emergency Relief Appropriation Act of 1935. Many congressmen believed that sovereign states had a responsibility to quarter their own militia. Changing their opinion required a new level of cooperation between the federal government and the states. An intense dialogue developed between the National Guard Association—one of the prime backers of the project in Washington—the National Guard Bureau, the state adjutants general, and sympathetic legislators. National Guard Association president and Illinois National Guard Major General Roy D. Keehn led the crusade and acted as coordinator.[21] In the view of the National Guard Association, the source of money for armories was provided in section 12 of the Emergency Relief Appropriation Act of 1935.

Applications for funding under the Act began at the local level. Municipalities submitted building plans, budgets, and information on local contributions to their state WPA office. The State of Missouri alone requested fifty armories, which reflected decades with a lack of support from the Missouri legislature. No armories had been built with state funds, aside from the state arsenal and armory at Jefferson City, since the 1880s.[22]

In April 1935, the subcommittees of the congressional Committees on Military Affairs held a joint hearing to discuss the use of federal funds to build armories for state National Guard units. There was little disagreement between members of the subcommittees and the witnesses called for testimony. Most repeated the same viewpoints about the utility, need, and legality of using public funds to build state armories. Keehn and the National Guard Association were most intent on earmarking a portion of the $5 billion Emergency Relief Act for the construction of Guard armories and other facilities. According to his figures, the National Guard was in dire need of 866 armories to be located in 810 communities scattered across the United States to house 1,740 units.

Testimony closed with a wealth of letters and telegrams from around the country supporting the plan to allot a certain sum for armory construction. Colonel J. S. Bersey of the Michigan National Guard made a final observation, reminding the subcommittees that prior to World War

18. National Guard Bureau, *Annual Report . . . , 1936*, 25.

19. Field, *Final Report on the WPA Program, 1935–1943*, 52.

20. Ibid., 47.

21. Roy D. Keehn to Harold W. Brown, January 28, 1935, Armory correspondence files, MMMH.

22. Harold W. Brown to Roy D. Keehn, February 14, 1935, Armory correspondence files, MMMH.

I and the National Defense Act of 1916, the states maintained National Guard units for their own security, but now the War Department determined the type of troops the states should maintain and the number allotted to each state based on national defense. His point was that in the old days of infantry, cavalry, and some horse-artillery, the state could rely on those forces for internal security when needed. But now a state might host a medical or quartermaster unit that was of less use to the state, but of great benefit to the nation. These extra units needed housing and the states were not able to accommodate them without some federal assistance.[23]

During these negotiations, the National Guard and the National Guard Association began promoting the armory as a public meeting place for use when the guard was not drilling. The Guard representatives borrowed a traditional unit practice, renting the drill hall for private or public events to pay armory expenses, as a carrot to sell funding armories to Congress. Keehn encouraged the adjutants general to press this point as a major benefit of the armory-building program.[24] In this way, a centuries-old militia/Guard practice became a new role for the armory in American life—the armory as community center.

While high-level planning was going on behind the scenes in Washington, in Missouri progress on plans to build new armories continued on the local level. Units around the state made tentative plans with city officials based on an estimated cost of $35,000 per armory. The City of Warrensburg reported that its Chamber of Commerce would provide a site for an armory free of cost to the state. If needed, the local state teachers college also offered a site on campus at no cost.[25]

A great deal of help was coming from local sources around the state. The town of Caruthersville was very anxious to begin building. The city independently developed its own armory plans and generously sent them to Adjutant General Brown for use elsewhere if needed. That Guard unit too had secured a site courtesy of the city.[26]

Around 1935, a two-page memorandum from the National Guard Bureau in Washington, "Suggestions for National Guard Armory Plans," was circulated to the state adjutants general.[27] The advice in the memorandum included the need for standardization to ensure economy of construction and adaptability so the armory could easily be converted to civilian use. The list of suggestions was impressive for its insight. It covered kitchens, locker rooms, heating, club rooms, drill halls, supply and storage areas, administrative offices, motor storage, and an indoor rifle range. Although standardization was stressed, the memo ended with a critical admonition. Architectural style and exterior treatment were to be "purely a matter of available material, taste and community influence." This perspective recognized the regional variations found within the borders of the United States. In later years, regional variation would be sacrificed on the altar of standardization, with less than satisfying results.

WPA officials began to take the armory program seriously by July 1935. General Keehn began promoting a comprehensive armory project that allotted $1,840,000 to the state of Missouri for the construction of forty-nine armories. Missouri did not receive that much federal aid, but it did put Missourians back to work building armories. From a National Guard perspective, the work of the WPA and PWA in Missouri was a success. Many unemployed Missourians were put to work

23. Statement of Colonel J. S. Bersey, Michigan National Guard, in US Congress, *Joint Hearing … Construction of National Guard Armories* (1935), 17.

24. Roy D. Keehn to Appropriations Committee, May 9, 1935, Armory correspondence files, MMMH.

25. Fred B. House to Harold W. Brown, June 20, 1935, Armory correspondence files, MMMH.

26. G. W. Phipps to Harold W. Brown, June 24, 1935, Armory correspondence files, MMMH.

27. US National Guard Bureau, "Suggestions for National Guard Armory Plans" ca. 1935, Type Sheet, National Guard Bureau folder, MMMH.

and the state received many new buildings for little expense. But buried in the bureaucracy was a series of inconsistencies about the armory program. Many towns that complied with Adjutant General Brown's instructions got their buildings, but many did not (see table 1, p. 102). For instance, municipalities that submitted complete proposals in December 1935 included Kirksville, Kennett, Sikeston, Doniphan, Warrensburg, and Columbia. These cities were approved and gained ownership of an armory. Other cities in the same circumstance that submitted their paperwork at the same time and had similar need for an armory were Chaffee, Fayette, Maryville, Mexico, Nevada, and Steele. Unfortunately, these cities received no reward for their efforts. Cities with incomplete paperwork in December 1935 that later succeeded in getting funding included Albany, Bernie, Cape Girardeau, Caruthersville, Chillicothe, Festus, Hannibal, and Neosho. Other municipalities, including Farmington, Jefferson City, Poplar Bluff, Springfield, and St. Joseph, apparently turned in no information. Two municipalities that did not submit complete information did receive armories—Sedalia and Dexter. Other towns, however, such as Monett, Boonville, Clinton, Carthage, Burlington Junction, and Lamar, did not receive an armory. The reasons behind individual decisions are unknown, but may include a change of city interest in pursuing the armory project, WPA deciding that a community already had a project, or a city waited too long and lost out when funding was redirected to other projects.

The WPA armories stand for a number of firsts in armory lore. The WPA legislation marked the first time the federal government became involved in armory construction, albeit in the guise of a back-to-work program. Federal financing ensured a certain amount of design uniformity in all WPA armories. The wealth of money unleashed from the public treasury caused an architectural proliferation of the modern armories. Because art deco and streamline moderne were the most popular building styles at the time and the armory construction program was nationwide, this era marks the first time armories were built in uniform styles from coast to coast. In addition, the armory construction program was promoted by a grassroots organization, the National Guard Association, which identified housing for National Guard units as a worthy relief cause, married it to a national need for jobs, and embarked on a national lobbying program that addressed both problems. For possibly the first time in militia/Guard history, a nongovernmental organization influenced a National Guard construction program, promoted it at the highest levels of political and military leadership, and succeeded in overcoming legal obstacles to see it become a reality. In the process, another use was found for the Guard armory and most WPA armories were also designed as community centers. A traditional but unofficial activity for armories before the Depression was now folded into the official mission of the armory building.

Every state in the Union experienced the WPA building craze. Due to the wide and overwhelming popularity of a limited number of architectural styles, art deco and the later WPA modern styles are the most recognized architectural styles in Missouri armories. The armories were also standardized according to price: buildings meant to house a company were allotted $25,000 and buildings meant to serve as a headquarters were allotted $75,000.

Another feature distinguishes the WPA armory from previous types; it acquired an additional function as a community center that grew in importance to equal its military role. Some art deco, streamline moderne, and PWA/WPA modern armories still service the National Guard, but others in the post–World War II years have become the property of their respective communities.

The Great Depression had forced society to adapt the armory again. The state and private wealth that had built militia castles around the turn of the century was replaced with national wealth. Cities and towns across America acquired novel designs because the bulk of the cost was paid by the national government, and the art deco style and its variants became the typical style for WPA projects in towns across the nation. The idea of the armory as community center goes back to the first armories of the volunteer militia when community use for private and civic purposes provided money to pay rents and upkeep. The Great Depression inserted the community center into the mainstream of armory mission and design, and the community center concept has remained synonymous with the armory ever since.

In retrospect, the WPA armories and community centers are among the most attractive and durable government buildings in Missouri. Just as locals learned to live with the castellated style, the community accepted the futuristic art deco armory and community center. Although the armories were designed according to a general plan, the WPA armories were able to fit in with the stock of main street buildings because their shapes and scale fit the town, and because community involvement in the project spurred acceptance.

Inventory of Art Deco/WPA Armories (by date built)

Fig. 4.3: 138th Infantry Regiment Armory, 1950
3676 Market Street, St. Louis
Style: WPA modern
Built 1937; occupied 1937–1971
Architect/builder: A. Osburg
Photo: MMMH

The St. Louis 138th Infantry Regiment Armory is a regimental-size armory still serving the St. Louis area community as a sports center, part of its original mission as a community center. This WPA project has art deco elements in a design style also known as civic monumental style. This armory was the home of the 138th Infantry Regiment from 1937 until 1971. The building was designed by architect A. Osburg and built in 1937 to replace a temporary 1908 armory on Grand Avenue. The Grand Avenue armory had been built for the First Regiment of Infantry as a temporary dwelling; thirty-one years later the unit was finally able to move into a permanent home. The new armory met the Guard unit's space requirements and provided construction jobs during the Great Depression in the St. Louis area. On May 15, 1934, the City of St. Louis approved a bond issue to fund improvements; $15 million of the bond issue, plus a 30 percent grant from the PWA, made construction of the $1,347,000 armory possible.[28] Several locations were considered, including expanding the site on Grand Avenue or moving to the uptown area on Grand Avenue near the site of Camp Jackson Plaza between Pine Street and Lawton Boulevard. Eventually a large lot on Market Street between Prospect and Bernard Avenues was chosen. The armory project on Market Street was almost scrapped several times by the PWA in 1935 and 1936, when the City of St. Louis experienced delays in selling bonds to fund its share of the armory cost.[29]

This armory is a large two-story building with a monitor-type roof over a large parade hall. The office wing at street level is constructed of a dark brown brick with stone trim. The roof of the office wing is flat with an elaborate tall smooth-dressed stone parapet. The primary entry is centered in a recessed area with ten-foot-tall limestone eagles in relief. At other locations in the pavilions, there are carved stone panels

28. "Historic 138th Regiment Taking Over New Armory," *St. Louis Post-Dispatch*, January 14, 1939.

29. "City Acts to Save Big PWA Grant on Proposed Armory," *St. Louis Post-Dispatch*, February 2, 1936.

with images of spread-winged eagles. Each corner is slightly enlarged to anchor the curtain walls with massive federal eagles on each facing side.

The entrance is massive with six brass doors and transoms under four courses of curved decorative stone, leading into a terrazzo-floored lobby. Over the outside doors is a Missouri state seal surmounted by a cement frieze with the lettering "138th Infantry, Missouri National Guard" and two 138th Infantry seals (St. Louis on a caparisoned charger), in turn surmounted by incised lettering "Armory."

Fig. 4.3a: Corner eagles, St. Louis 138th Infantry Regiment Armory (Photo: MMMH)

Striking in overall size, the interior of the St. Louis armory conveys the classic form and size of a regimental armory more often found in the eastern United States. Facing the 142-by-258-foot drill hall (36,636 square feet of open space) are regimental and company offices and second-floor locker and supply rooms. The roof of the drill hall has skylights and is eighty-three feet above the drill floor; 134 floodlights hang from the ceiling at seventy-five feet above the drill floor. Walls above an encircling balcony are concrete blocks with glazed yellow tile below. The 138th insignia is a theme worked into the reviewing stand handrail.

Fig. 4.3b: Main door, St. Louis 138th Infantry Regiment Armory (Photo: MMMH)

The basement is large, with a 160-by-200-foot garage area for fifty cars surrounded by storage and utility rooms, a small arms range, handball courts, swimming pool, and officers' mess, clubroom, and large kitchen. The main floor holds a large officers' hall and workrooms. A regimental hall is on the second floor with trophy cases, library, and band room.[30]

The St. Louis Market Street armory illustrates a contradiction in National Guard goals and armory buildings. At one time, the Guard built armories to last many generations, but through the years a change in mission changed the life expectancy of the armory building. What was considered permanent in 1939 was abandoned by the Missouri Guard in 1971 for the "old mess hall" at Jefferson Barracks. After a thirty-four-year life, barely exceeding the life of the First Regiment's temporary home on Grand Avenue, the parent organization responsible for building the Market Street Armory declared it surplus in December 1971. The City of St. Louis, as part owner, had earlier received full ownership of the building and deeded it to the state in 1962.[31] The building was not without value: in 1987, the estimated value of the property and building was nearly $3.3 million or more. At a sale the same year, the building was sold to a private party for $250,100.[32]

30. *Historical Annual: National Guard of the State of Missouri, 1939*, ix.

31. "Handball, Soccer Games Keep Old Armory Busy," *St. Louis Post-Dispatch*, June 10, 1985.

32. "Armory Building's Sale Is Postponed in Suit Over Funds," *St. Louis Post-Dispatch*, June 25, 1987.

Fig. 4.4: Admiral Robert E. Coontz Armory, 1939
301 Collier Street, Hannibal, Marion County
Style: WPA modern
Built 1938; occupied 1939–1977
Architect/builder: Harold L. Reeder
Photo: MMMH

The armory in Hannibal was built by the WPA in 1938 in the WPA modern style. It was the home of Company L, 138th Infantry and named after US Navy Admiral Robert E. Coontz, the highest ranking military officer hailing from Hannibal.

If this armory had been constructed in monolithic cement, it would be closer to art deco in style, but due to the close proximity of quarry stone and surplus labor, the armory was finished in stone that was meant to match a rock wall in a nearby athletic park. The armory was built under the WPA program in part because the city donated the lot for the armory adjacent to a city ballpark.[33]

Quarry activity began some time before construction was started on January 24, 1938. Few of the 130 men employed in the construction knew how to work stone; therefore, the project took a long time. Because part of the reason for the construction project was to put men to work, each person worked only three days a week in order to spread the work around to as many families as possible. Laborers were paid 30 cents an hour, and the total cost for the structure was $85,000. The City of Hannibal contributed $25,000, the state $6,000, and the WPA $54,400.[34] The building was completed on November 4, 1939, and became home to Company L, 138th Infantry.

In 1944, the property surrounding the armory was used to house German prisoners of war, who worked sorting shoes that could be repaired and shipped to Europe for war refugees. The Guard remained in this armory until the current Hannibal Armory was completed in 1977. The Coontz Armory reverted to the city and is now part of the Hannibal Parks and Recreation system.

33. Sinclair Mainland to Guy B. Park, August 21, 1935, Armory correspondence files, MMMH.
34. "Armory a Tribute to Hannibal Native," *Hannibal Courier-Post*, March 2, 1996.

Fig. 4.5: Columbia National Guard Armory, 1940
701 East Ash Street, Columbia, Boone County
Style: art deco
Built 1938; occupied 1938–1996
Architect/builder: Deering and Clark
Photo: Dave Clark

The Columbia National Guard Armory is a product of a local, state, and federal effort to work together under the WPA program. Designed by local architects Robert B. Deering and Dave Clark and structural engineer R. B. B. Moorman, it was built in 1940 with WPA funding and occupied by the 128th Field Artillery until they moved to a new armory in 1996, at which time the building was converted into a city recreation facility (known as the Armory Sports and Recreation Center). The Columbia Armory was listed in the National Register of Historic Places in 1993.

Possibly the most compact of all the art deco and WPA armories, the Columbia Armory encompasses all the attributes of the style. When originally designed by Deering and Clark, the building was to be a brick-and-steel truss structure. A delay between adoption of the plan and the start of construction permitted the change to monolithic concrete, which served to keep the cost down. According to the architects, the total cost of the armory was about $112,000, a cost of thirty-two cents per cubic foot.[35]

The entire building was constructed of reinforced, poured concrete using the technique called architectural or monolithic concrete. The WPA consulted with the Portland Cement Company for technical advice in mixing gravel, sand, cement mix, and water. WPA workers required special training in how to pour large walls of cement and join individual pourings of three-and-a-half-foot lifts each. Joints between the lifts were carefully minimized and evenly spaced to keep the walls in character with cement as a building material.[36] Exterior surfaces were rubbed with stone to remove excess cement material at joints to increase the textured cement appearance.

The Columbia Armory building presents a clean exterior design: windows are in pairs to maintain symmetry, the main entrance is centered, and each side of the armory has a door or entryway. The main entrance (on the south side of the building) is the most ornate exterior treatment on the building facade. Flanking the double-door entrance are one-story piers with minimal embellishments. The piers have deeply incised lines around the top portions that give them a vague resemblance to inverted shell casings; some Guardsmen assumed this to be an intentional tribute to the artillery unit housed at the armory.

---

35. Deering, "Armory for Columbia, Missouri."
36. Ibid.

Centered above the door in the cornice frieze are the raised letters "ARMORY." The art deco ornamentation is clearly apparent, as is the uniform light color scheme that allows light and shadow to accent the building's curves and angles.

Fig. 4.5a: "Weaving" the Columbia lamellar roof, ca. 1939 (Photo: Dave Clark)

The side entrance on the east is the double-door entryway; the northern entry (on the rear of the building) is a single door reached by a metal fire escape stairway. The western entrance is a vehicle door opening into a basement garage. Only one chimney stack is visible on the armory roof; it is square with a recessed water channel around the air vent leading to drains on each corner. Each corner has an extension that acts as a "drip" to carry water away from the stack.

All building embellishments were hand crafted on the work site. Exterior decorations are primarily accents on prominent surfaces, including incised lines, geometric forms, and angles that are simple and crisp.[37] All curves, buttresses, beams, friezes, and minor ornamentation are concrete. Around the roofline is a horizontal frieze of repeating squares with a subtle drip line under the eve. Above the main door on the roofline is another frieze of truncated conical shapes. Surmounting the main doorway is the armory flagstaff. The flagstaff base is a concrete corbel with concentric geometric designs. Interior decoration consists of ornamental corbels at the roof and beam junctions and accent lines around the drill hall entrance.

The weight of the roof of the drill hall is carried on four concrete beams that extend from the ceiling junction through the main floor and into the subfloor of the basement level. The roof is a vault with a black asphalt covering. It was originally covered was a bright red/orange roll roofing that contrasted with the beige color of the entire armory exterior.[38] The ceiling employs the lamellar roofing system, in this case made up of 450 wood lamellae bolted in place.

A common observation about many WPA armories is that they were built in depressed neighborhoods for a reason: the armory was meant to intimidate the poor. The Columbia Armory appears to affirm that idea. The Columbia Armory is located north of the Boone County Courthouse and is adjacent to public housing and small businesses, but photographs of the area during the 1940 construction reveal a scattering of middle-income dwellings and the site, selected by the City of Columbia, was part of a commercial metal yard in 1935. A more probable reason for locating the armory so near the county courthouse is simply the availability of space. The City of Columbia owned the lot and donated it as part of their proposal to the WPA to secure funding for the armory.

37. Klein and Fogle, *Clues to American Architecture*, 50–51.

38. Dave Clark to Robert P. Wiegers, personal communication, 1992.

Fig. 4.6: Company C, 735th Support Battalion Armory, 1997
401 West Walnut, Doniphan, Ripley County
Style: WPA modern
Built 1938; occupied 1938–present
Architect/builder: Hal Lynch
Photo: Chuck MacFall

The WPA armory in Doniphan does not fit into the art deco style because of the river stone used for the exterior wall treatment in a style called Ozark Rock. This type of style, using elements of modern style, but lacking art deco ornamentation and built using local materials, is grouped into a separate category called WPA modern.

Construction of the Doniphan armory was a community effort that began in 1935 in response to a recommendation from the state adjutant general that a new armory in Doniphan would increase enlistments in the area. According to Captain Albert D. Sheppard, commander of Company I, 140th Infantry, the Doniphan Chamber of Commerce had already purchased a site for the armory at a cost of $675; the site was to be deeded to the state when the project was completed.[39] Final funding for the armory included a $1,753 local contribution and $33,881 from the federal government.[40]

Construction on the armory began on August 22, 1938, using sandstone from the nearby Current River for the building exterior. River sandstone was not a typical medium for WPA buildings. National practice was to build in monolithic cement, but local builders in the Ozark region were accustomed to using this stone. The armory is still used as a community center and as home to Company C (Detachment 2), 735th Support Battalion.

39. Albert D. Sheppard to Harold W. Brown, November 15, 1935, Armory correspondence files, MMMH.

40. Fred C. Richmond to Harold W. Brown, December 16, 1935, Armory correspondence files, MMMH.

Fig. 4.7: Former Company E, 140th Infantry Armory, 1997
Electric Street, Kennett, Dunklin County
Style: WPA modern
Built 1938; occupied 1940–1986
Architect/builder: J. A. Sutterfield
Photo: Chuck MacFall

Fig. 4.8: Former Battery B, 129th Field Artillery Armory, 1997
1500 Washington, Chillicothe, Livingston County
Style: art deco
Built 1938; occupied 1940–1996
Architect/builder: R. Robert Warren
Photo: Chuck MacFall

Fig. 4.9: Clyde Burdick American Legion Armory, 1997
Brooks and Jefferson Streets, Neosho, Newton County
Style: WPA modern
Built 1938; occupied 1938–ca. 2000
Architect/builder: George Draper
Photo: Chuck MacFall

Fig. 4.10: Headquarters Company, Thirty-fifth Division Armory, ca. 1950
Holden Street, Warrensburg, Johnson County
Style: WPA modern
Built 1938; occupied 1938–1954 (building burned)
Architect/builder unknown
Photo: MMMH

Fig. 4.11: Lt. Patrick H. Adams Memorial Armory, 1997
300 South Main Street, Sikeston, Scott County
Style: WPA modern
Built 1938–39; occupied 1939–present
Architect/builder: J. A. Sutterfield
Photo: Chuck MacFall

The armory in Sikeston includes elements of the modern style, but is built in traditional red brick rather than monolithic cement. Construction on the 19,600-square-foot armory began in 1938 on land donated to the state on May 24 of that year.[41] Along with the transfer came a controversy that would surface several years later. The land had been owned by heirs of the locally prominent Matthews family, who had donated the land to the city for use as a park. The city, in turn, deeded a portion of the park to the State of Missouri for an armory.

Construction of the armory was headed by C. M. Taylor, superintendent for the WPA, using a design by J. A. Sutterfield of Sikeston. The armory was built at a cost of approximately $53,000, with the state furnishing about $8,300, the city $16,000, and the WPA the remainder. The armory was completed in the early part of 1939. Inside the armory are a 10,200-square-foot drill floor, various offices, assembly rooms, and a banquet room capable of seating three hundred people.[42]

In the mid-1950s, a dispute arose between the City of Sikeston and the Missouri Guard over which party had control over the actual armory building and who could authorize use of the armory facility. In this case, the Guard requested the US Army Reserve, a temporary user of the armory, to find quarters elsewhere due to space considerations, but the city felt the Guard had no authority to order anyone out without city approval. In early 1958, at a meeting between the three groups, a local alderman claimed that the National Guard was basically telling the city council that management of the armory did not concern it.[43] Eventually, the armory question was solved through an agreement with Adjutant General Sheppard.[44]

Fig. 4.11a: Aerial photo Sikeston, ca. 1940. The armory and adjoining park are at the center. (Photo: MMMH)

41. General Warranty Deed from City of Sikeston to the State of Missouri, May 24, 1938, Armory correspondence files, MNGFE.

42. "Sikeston's New Armory Will Soon Be Completed," *Sikeston* (MO) *Herald*, February 2, 1939.

43. "Alderman Keller Charges Guard Says Management of Armory Not City's Business," *Daily Sikeston Standard*, January 21, 1958.

44. "All's Well That Ends Well," *Daily Sikeston Standard*, January 22, 1958.

Fig. 4.12: A. C. Brase Arena Community Center/former Headquarters, 140th Infantry Armory, ca. 1960

410 Kiwanis Drive, Cape Girardeau, Cape Girardeau County

Style: art deco

Built 1939; occupied 1939–1957

Architect/builder: Hal Lynch and J. Carl Jourdan

Photo: MMMH

This armory served the state for a brief eighteen-year period, five years of which were part of World War II, only to be decommissioned in 1957. After the Guard departed, the building found another life as a parks and recreation/community center. When this armory was built, it was intended to serve also as a community center. Now the building serves that alternate purpose exclusively as the A. C. Brase Arena Community Center.

This armory was designed by Hal Lynch and J. Carl Jourdan in 1937. The City of Cape Girardeau requested that the armory be located on a lot in the city park in the best part of town, and be a size and value of $75,000 instead of the ordinary $25,000 size.[45] Both the city and the Missouri National Guard wanted the larger building, each for its own reasons. Chamber of Commerce president H. I. Himmelberger, representing the city, wanted the economic benefits that would come with having a larger armory with many units assigned there, whereas the Missouri Guard felt the size of the city (18,000 at that time) and its regional prominence could support the enlistment of enough good quality men to form three units. To attain this end, F. A. Pfeffer, chairman of the city National Guard Armory Committee, stated that the city was willing to deed land in the park to the state and guarantee a contribution of $2,500 to the project.[46]

This armory was only occupied for a few years before the start of World War II as headquarters of the 140th Infantry. During the war, a state Guard unit occupied the building. In the

Fig. 4.12a: Outdoor seating area at the Brase Arena (formerly the Cape Girardeau armory) (Photo: Wiegers)

45. Percy R. Little to Harold W. Brown, August 31, 1935, Armory correspondence files, MMMH.
46. F. A. Pfeffer to Harold W. Brown, December 12, 1935, Armory correspondence files, MMMH.

postwar years, the auditorium foyer was converted into two floors to provide additional office space for unit guardsmen.[47] As part of the reorganization of the National Guard during the Cold War, a new Cape Girardeau armory was completed in 1957.

Currently the Brase Arena is located in a park-like setting with a well-maintained interior and exterior. The community center retains many of the features built into the original armory, such as the drill hall floor, bench seating, kitchen, and a stage. It has a unique feature at the rear of the building: concrete outdoor bleachers that originally faced the County Fairgrounds and now front a track and ball fields. The Cape Girardeau Armory was the only art deco/WPA armory in the state to include attached outside seating, a reflection of the concept of providing a community center and park/fairgrounds setting for the original armory.

Fig. 4.13: Monett Civic Center/former 203rd Coast Artillery Armory, 1997
205 Euclid, Monett, Barry County
Style: WPA modern
Built 1939; occupied 1939–1992
Architect/builder unknown
Photo: Chuck MacFall

47. "140th Infantry Quarters Remodeled."

Fig. 4.14: Company B, 140th Infantry Armory, 1997
801 West Third Street, Caruthersville, Pemiscot County
Style: WPA modern
Built ca. 1939; occupied 1939–ca. 2000
Architect: Hal Lynch / Builder: S. C. Stevens
Photo: Chuck MacFall

This armory was built as a WPA project and incorporates many aspects of the WPA modern style inside and out, but the stylistic features are somewhat extreme and could not be considered typical of the art deco style. This is illustrated in the two pillars flanking the main entrance and the lack of geometric ornamentation.

Fig. 4.15: Joe E. Grohs Jr. Community Center/former Company M, 140th Infantry Armory, 1998
215 North Mill Street, Festus, Jefferson County
Style: art deco
Built 1939; occupied 1941–1991
Architect/builder: Hal Lynch
Photo: Chuck MacFall

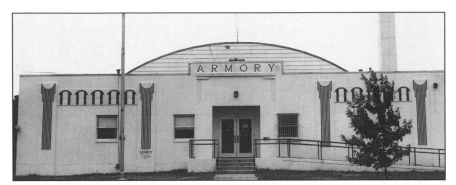

Fig. 4.16: Company C, 735th Support Battalion Armory, 1997

503 Walnut, Bernie, Stoddard County

Style: art deco

Built 1940; occupied 1940–ca. 1999

Architect: J. A. Sutterfield / Builder unknown

Photo: Chuck MacFall

The Bernie Armory was designed for a single Guard company, but over the years, the building has been home to numerous Guard units. The Bernie city attorney was able to report in 1935 that the community had purchased a one-and-a-half-acre site valued at $800 for $225, and that publicity about the project had raised great expectations for the new armory.[48] The estimated cost of the armory was $40,000.[49] The Bernie community provided $5,000 needed to build the structure and to ensure its use as a high school gym. The Guard left the armory in the late 1990s. The building is currently a community center.

Fig. 4.17: Aurora School District Office/former Company M, 203rd Coast Artillery Armory, 1997

409 West Locust Street, Aurora, Lawrence County

Style: art deco

Built 1940; occupied 1944–1992

Architect/builder: Besecke-Swanson-Terney

Photo: Chuck MacFall

48. C. Black to Harold W. Brown, November 15, 1935, Armory correspondence files, MMMH.

49. "Southeast Missouri News," *Malden Merit*, January 5, 1940.

The former Aurora armory is currently the offices of the Aurora School District. This art deco armory is one of the most imposing armory buildings in the state. It was built in 1940 and once housed Company M, Second Regiment. Above the recessed doorways are bas-reliefs, deeply carved panels with a stylized spread-winged eagle motif.

This armory, like other WPA armories, was a joint venture between the federal government, the Missouri National Guard, and the City of Aurora. In August 1940, the WPA approved the armory project and architects Besecke-Swanson-Terney of Jefferson City designed it for the community and Guard use. Some of the earliest plans called for a separate auditorium wing, but this section is not evident in the building today. Instead, the gymnasium has doubled as the auditorium, as in other armories. In addition to the planned auditorium, there were numerous offices and a meeting hall set aside for local groups and organizations. The plan also contained offices for the Aurora school district. The architects originally estimated the cost of the building to be $199,000 of which the City of Aurora was expected to pay $69,000, the Guard was expected to pay $10,000, and the State Board of Education was expected to come up with $2,000. The WPA would fund the rest. The city passed a bond issue for $20,000 in 1940 to raise funds for their portion of the cost.[50] Then, in December 1940, President Roosevelt announced a cutback in non-war-related building projects. Aurora citizens began to fear that the armory that was to meet their needs for years to come might be halted despite all their work and financial support.[51] In order to avoid a delay, the armory was reduced in size to stay within the original cost estimate as the start-up of defense projects drove up the prices of building materials. The floor plan was reduced and the height of the building was lowered over the drill hall and auditorium building.[52] But in June 1941, a question arose about the priorities for the different planned uses of the building and how they related to what the city wanted and what the WPA was building. In letters between the WPA district manager and the adjutant general, the Guard clarified its position on the priorities in construction. The City of Aurora wanted the auditorium finished first or simultaneously with the armory. Pointing out that the WPA projects were focused on building armories that also had facilities for use by the community and that the armory was the top priority, Adjutant General Means informed the city that "if additional funds are required in order to construct the theatre section, such additional funds shall be furnished by the Sponsor prior to the commencement of operations on the theatre section of this building." The reason the Guard took this hard position is that the adjutant general's office believed the estimate for the cost per cubic foot was too low and if the money ran out it should be the theatre/auditorium that was not completed, not the armory.[53]

The city refused to accept the Guard's interpretation of the priorities for the construction project. Prior to the armory project the community had given "its undivided attention to other public projects, mainly school buildings."[54] The city wanted an armory only if the state and WPA paid most of the cost. According to Mayor Cowan, the city had no authority to accept a priority for an armory only. The city believed the bond issue had been voted on for construction of an auditorium and armory and office building and it was prepared to go to court on the issue. Cowan wrote, "As far as the City Council is concerned, this whole project can be dropped if the armory building priority is the final word."[55] The armory stands today as evidence the city did not drop the project and file a claim, but it is unknown why the city demurred and what accommodation was made to finish the auditorium.

Completion of the armory was a long drawn-out affair. War necessities and priorities drew resources away from domestic construction. Even prior to December 7, 1941, the WPA director of operations for District #1, Guy Lloyd, was attempting to find out why the project could not purchase supplies.[56] In the post–Pearl Harbor emergency, the construction situation continued to deteriorate. The Aurora armory

50. "Long Hoped for Armory is Now Near Reality," *Aurora Advertiser*, October 17, 1940.

51. "Believe Armory Is Not to Be Held Up by the New Ruling," *Aurora Advertiser*, December 12, 1940.

52. R. D. Cowan to Guy L. Lloyd, February 25, 1941, Armory correspondence files, MMMH.

53. Lewis M. Means to John M. McCann, June 11, 1941, Armory correspondence files, MMMH.

54. Lloyd G. Stark to Harold W. Brown, November 21, 1935, Armory correspondence files, MMMH.

55. R. D. Cowan to Guy L. McCann, June 11, 1941, Armory correspondence files, MMMH.

56. Guy L. Lloyd to V. W. Whitfield, September 17, 1941, Armory correspondence files, MMMH.

project was closed down in September 1942 for lack of cement and lamellar roof material. Carpenters and other skilled laborers were now resources allotted to jobs as needed. Architects were now making "some changes that could be made to save critical materials." All these decisions were being made in an atmosphere of economic constriction. State money not committed before December 31 would revert to the general fund. With the war years ahead, no one knew when new funding would be available to finish an armory.[57]

The main building of the complex was finished as an armory. The building has not changed since it was finished in 1944, except in the interior. It was remodeled in the early 1990s to add extra space for classrooms and modernize the gym for the Aurora public schools. Today the building is owned entirely by the Aurora School District.

Fig. 4.18: Colonel James E. Rieger Armory, 1997
500 South Elson Street, Kirksville, Adair County
Style: art deco
Built 1940; occupied 1942–present
Architect/builder: Irwin Dunbar
Photo: Chuck MacFall

The Kirksville Armory is the most impressive Guard-owned armory in Missouri. It was designed by Irwin Dunbar in the late 1930s and is a prime example of art deco in Missouri. The building was dedicated in 1942 as the Colonel James E. Rieger Armory and Community Center, named for a local veteran who had been cited several times for bravery in World War I and received the Distinguished Service Cross for action in France.

The main entry to the building has a tall window opening above it and in a frieze above that is incised the word "armory" and, most dramatically, a bas-relief of a spread-winged eagle. The warranty deed for land at 500 South Elson Street was filed on June 17, 1938, and the armory was completed in 1940. The dedication ceremony was held March 6, 1942, for the first armory completed since the declaration of war.

The community supported the WPA project in a variety of ways and one reason the Kirksville Armory

57. Fred C. Horan to E. B. Flinn, September 28, 1942, Armory correspondence files, MMMH.

made it to the construction stage was the backing of the community and the quick thinking of the local armory committee. Kirksville was one of the first communities to have a proposal prepared by a local architect and have the drawings and sketches approved by the WPA district office in Moberly and the state WPA director. The city sponsored the WPA proposal and Adair County and the Kirksville Special Road District furnished all tools necessary for construction. The local school board donated the armory site, one square city block only four blocks from the courthouse and business district. The land was valued between $4,000 to $8,000; for legal purposes, it was purchased by the Chamber of Commerce, which sold it to the state for $100. The city employed local architect Irwin Dunbar to design the project.[58]

The City of Kirksville was ready to start the building in 1938, but actual construction did not commence until August 1940. The year-long delay can be attributed to dramatic changes in the overall project and limitations placed on nonlabor costs.[59] The original plan called for a small brick armory to be built at a cost of $36,056. The sponsor, the City of Kirksville, proposed changing the plans to substitute a reinforced concrete building, which necessitated submitting superseding documentation to the WPA. The change was approved for what amounted to a second project, using the same location but a different structure.

When the altered plans for the armory were approved, the cost stood at $129,125. Most of this budget increase was due to the use of new construction techniques and the addition of office space requested by the city. In addition to the six National Guard units and detachments posted to the armory, the county planned to have the armory house offices for a variety of county agencies, the Triple A Program (Agricultural Adjustment Administration), the county agent, the local office of the Missouri Health Department, and the local state forester.

Eventually the project ran out of money and construction ground to a halt. Project superintendent James B. Tharp wrote to the WPA district director in Moberly, "This job is drageing [sic] as far as time is concerned, and it is 90% the Sponsors [sic] fault."[60] But others believed that the sponsor and Adair County had contributed to or exceeded their agreed amount, and it was widely acknowledged "there has been no mismanagement in this project which has been going on since 1937 and very little waste." The project was simply a victim of a reviving economy in which prices were rising for materials and labor; this was a good moment for the economy, but a bad moment for the construction project. As late as May 26, 1941, the project needed an additional $5,000 to finish the building. The city had paid several times the amount it had promised and Adair County had met its commitment. The unit commander Major Wray M. Rieger was forced to write congressmen in an effort to secure more funding to complete the building.[61]

Today, the Kirksville Armory still houses a National Guard unit. Over the years, there have been few changes to the building, inside or out. The most noticeable adaptation is the glass blocks in the front façade that were added in the 1960s. The armory has never had a motor pool area and thus howitzers and trucks are stored at a secure storage area nearby.

58. Nathaniel B. Rieger to Harold W. Brown, November 16, 1935, Armory correspondence files, MMMH.

59. B. M. Casteel to Francis H. Dryden, June 24, 1941, Armory correspondence files, MMMH.

60. James B. Tharp to Swan McDonald, April 23, 1941, Armory correspondence files, MMMH.

61. Wray M. Rieger to M. A. Romjue, May 26, 1941, Armory correspondence files, MMMH.

Fig. 4.19: 1138th Military Police Company Armory, 1998
1315 Webster, West Plains, Howell County
Style: WPA modern
Built 1940; occupied 1941–present
Architect/builder: Hal Lynch
Photo: Chuck MacFall

Fig. 4.20: Battery A, 129th Field Artillery Armory, ca. 1950
411 North College, Albany, Gentry County
Style: WPA modern
Built 1941; occupied 1941–present
Architect/builder: Joseph Shaughnessy
Photo: MMMH

The Albany armory demonstrates the complexity in the WPA category. This large armory building was funded and built by the WPA. The brick building has muted classical revival details and a pronounced art deco–style sign over the entrance. Other than the sign over the entrance, the building lacks other art deco elements, and it was built of brick rather than of monolithic cement; therefore, this building is not representative of the typical art deco armory.

Fig. 4.21: Company C, Sixth Regiment Armory, 1998
105 East North Main Street, Dexter, Stoddard County
Style: streamline moderne
Built 1941; occupied 1942–2006
Architect/builder: Hal Lynch
Photo: Chuck MacFall

The Dexter armory was designed by Hal Lynch and built in 1941 with WPA funding. It is considered a WPA modern armory because of its funding, but the design has strong horizontal incised lines, placing it in the streamline moderne style, in contrast to the more vertical lines of the art deco style. The façade is symmetrical with three recessed single-leaf door entries. Above the left entry are the incised letters, NATIONAL GUARD, and on the right entry CITY HALL. The entry, a double-leaf door with sidelights topped by a transom window, is centered, and above the door is a frieze in which the words CITY OF DEXTER are incised.

When the armory was first considered in 1939, it received an immediate boost from the local American Legion post, which proposed the WPA project and donated land to get it started.[62] The local community contributed several thousand dollars for the project and expected a federal grant of $30,000 to build the armory and community center. The WPA eventually provided nearly $60,000 in supplies and labor for the project,

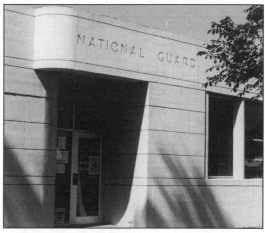

Fig. 4.21a: Incised "National Guard" over left entry door (Photo: Wiegers)

the State of Missouri added $7,500, and the City of Dexter committed $12,000. Within seven months, work began on the new armory, and by January 1941, the foundation had been poured and the building was ready for construction.[63] Seventeen months later, in June 1942, Company C and city officials were able to move into the new armory/city hall.

The completed building held an 8,500-square-foot drill hall that could seat nearly two thousand people. In addition, the Guard section of the building was built with lockers, showers, an officers' room, office space, and a vault for guns and ammunition with a large storeroom on the first floor.[64] In addition to the Guard's portion of the armory, areas were designed for the Missouri Highway Patrol and city administration offices. The building is currently a community center.

62. "Legion Investigates Means of Building Armory and Arena," *Dexter Statesman*, June 23, 1939.

63. "Armory Building Proposed for Dexter," *Dexter Statesman*, July 28, 1939.

64. "City Office and Guard Co. Moved to Armory," *Dexter Statesman*, June 26, 1942.

Fig. 4.22: Company C, 1140th Engineer Battalion Armory, 1997
701 South Main, Charleston, Mississippi County
Style: streamline moderne
Built 1941; occupied 1941–ca. 2005
Architect: Hal Lynch / Builder: Philips and Assoc.
Photo: Chuck MacFall

In comparison to art deco, which emphasized linear composition, geometric designs, and vertical massing, the low profile and horizontal incising on the façade of the armory in Charleston are characteristic of the streamline moderne style.

Fig. 4.23: Major General John C. McLaughlin Armory, 1998
100 West and Ninth Street, Sedalia, Pettis County
Style: art deco
Built 1941; occupied 1944–2003
Architect/builder unknown
Photo: Chuck MacFall

Fig. 4.24: Company F, 140th Infantry, 1997
820 North Fifth Street, Poplar Bluff, Butler County
Style: WPA modern
Built 1942; occupied 1942–1997
Architect/builder: E. C. Thomas
Photo: Chuck MacFall

The Poplar Bluff armory is a WPA modern building with subtle classical elements. It was built in 1942 by the WPA on plans from architect E. C. Thomas. The City of Poplar Bluff was interested in securing an armory for their city and donated through the Community Club a one-acre lot worth $3,000 only four blocks from the business district.[65] Altogether the city pledged $7,377.50 toward the armory project. By July 1940, forty-two men were employed on the armory project, building 6,000 large blocks for the outside walls on the front lawn of the building site.[66] The income from the state labor was a welcome addition to the local economy. The project was supervised by WPA and state officials. Currently the building is the Poplar Bluff R-1 School District maintenance and warehouse building.

65. O. C. Cutsinger to Harold W. Brown, November 22, 1935, Armory correspondence files, MMMH.

66. "Construction of Armory and Community Building Is Moving Along with Exceptional Speed," *Daily American Republic*, July 20, 1940.

Table 1: Building costs of proposed WPA armories in Missouri, by county

County	Town	Federal Funds	Sponsor's Funds	Total Cost	Town Population
Adair	Kirksville	55,298.00	2,200.00	57,498.00	7,213
Audrain	Mexico	38,190.00	3,325.00	41,515.00	8,290
Boone	Columbia	55,000.00	7,600.00	62,600.00	10,392
Butler	Poplar Bluff	25,843.50	3,388.05	29,231.55	7,551
Cole	Jefferson City	25,000.00	11,912.75	36,912.75	21,596
Dunklin	Kennett	32,570.60	1,970.00	34,540.60	4,128
Gentry	Albany	26,973.20	2,500.00	29,473.20	1,858
Howard	Fayette	30,982.00	3,543.00	34,525.00	2,630
Howell	West Plains	25,980.15	2,026.10	28,006.25	3,335
Jefferson	Festus	32,373.35	4,370.00	36,743.35	4,085
Johnson	Warrensburg	24,998.30	6,795.81	31,794.11	5,146
Livingston	Chillicothe	32,252.00	5,133.00	37,385.00	6,672
Marion	Hannibal	24,718.40	7,700.00	32,418.40	19,306
Mississippi	Charleston	15,333.01	2,667.00	18,000.01	3,410
New Madrid	Marston	26,528.62	1,176.10	27,704.72	350
Newton	Neosho	21,860.45	4,025.00	25,885.45	3,968
Nodaway	Maryville	9,815.52	90.00	9,905.52	5,215
Pemiscot	Caruthersville	26,604.62	1,476.10	28,080.72	4,750
Pemiscot	Steele	26,528.62	1,176.10	27,704.72	1,219
Ripley	Doniphan	33,881.10	1,753.00	35,634.10	1,398
St. Francois	Farmington	47,228.10	1,720.00	48,948.10	3,001
St. Louis	Robertson	20,885.50	4,255.00	25,140.50	——
Scott	Chaffee	27,201.90	1,179.55	28,381.45	3,035
Scott	Sikeston	26,204.52	2,667.00	28,871.52	5,676
Stoddard	Bernie	24,372.50	2,143.00	26,515.50	4,031
Stoddard	Dexter	27,744.75	1,931.25	29,676.00	2,714
Vernon	Nevada	30,304.45	4,370.00	34,674.45	7,448
Buchanan	St. Joseph	189,827.65	11,155.00	200,982.65	80,934
	TOTAL	**984,500.81**	**104,247.81**	**1,088,748.62**	

Source: MMMH Archives, Folder March 1936.

Chapter 5
Cold War Armories
The Midcentury Modern and Type 783 Category

Demobilization after World War II was not as sweeping as it had been after World War I due to the onset of the Cold War. The growing standoff between East and West necessitated a defense establishment unheard of in peacetime America. Most industrialized countries could meet the need for a larger defense establishment simply by enhancing their regular army. But in America, the maintenance of a large army was contrary to the national tradition of a small army; therefore, the only recourse was to rely on the Army Reserve and the states' National Guard units for additional manpower.

An enhanced National Guard required a larger pool of armories to house them. Prior to the war, armory design was based on the accumulated experiences handed down from vernacular, castellated, and the WPA modern styles. The U-shaped drill hall with offices on three sides was an efficient use of space, and popular regional variations were incorporated into the WPA armory without undermining the principle of standardization. The community center concept also passed the test of time and was successfully built into the armory floor plan without detriment to the mission. All in all, most Guard leaders expected to see armories built after 1945 that would continue the prewar model of state/federal cost sharing and would probably continue the WPA styles with some new and modern twists. But modernist architecture entered a new phase after the war (often called midcentury modern), which affected the basic interpretation of what an armory should look like, as reflected in designs that still stand out today. Congressional action also contributed to a transformation from earlier armory construction styles, which allowed regional variations, to the rigidity of the new midcentury style in armory design. The earlier floor plan was retained, but the standardization of style almost eliminated regional variation. The highly successful community center concept of the 1930s was greatly reduced so that the prominent stage included in the prewar floor plan disappeared altogether. The result was a building that eliminated the best of the modern movement in exchange for promoting utility and low cost.

Modern architecture, often called 1950s modern, American imperial modern, or postmodernist, held great promise for a new direction in building and promoted itself as the best building for the money. In this study, the variant of modernism that preoccupied architects from 1945 to 1973 is called modern, a confusing word since it is used to describe manufactured items, a current life style, and a time period. However, it can also mean "modern architecture," a movement that began in the late nineteenth to early twentieth century and continues into the present. In American architecture, the modernist period represents the triumph of pure form and function over traditional styles and materials.[1] The obsession with efficiency and uniform materials was spurred on by the 1930s infatuation with machines and engineering simplicity. The same mechanical infatuation that propelled the WPA styles was transformed into a new phase of the modern movement.

The dominant concept in modern architecture was to eliminate ornamentation as a way to emphasize the form of the structure. This goal was accomplished with recently developed types of glass, steel, and concrete and by embracing the innovative idea of matching cost to production. With the previous international style and modernist style that evolved from it, efficiency triumphed over symbolism, structure, and function in the American cityscape.[2] Much of the official enthusiasm for the modern design was based on a fundamental notion that modern building techniques could produce a building more efficiently and cheaper than traditional styles. Theoretically, the new modern armory would complement neighboring buildings in any size community.[3] Compounding this notion was the modern view that the simplified form, without decoration, was universally applicable to all people, regardless of climate, continent, or culture.[4]

The leading proponents of the modern style in the postwar years were Walter Gropius, Le Corbusier, Ludwig Mies van der Rohe, and Eero Saarinen. Some of these Europeans immigrated to the United States where they taught that the new world order needed modernism to build better housing detached from the unorganized, traditional city of neighborhoods. In Europe and Asia, vast tracts of traditional housing were destroyed by war, but in America the wrecking ball and bulldozer stood in for enemy bombs. Acres of housing were leveled to build a modern living space under the guise of urban redevelopment, guided by modern theories of tall towers and planned green spaces.[5] In 1955, St. Louis succumbed to modern housing theory and condemned acres of mixed vernacular housing to build the Pruitt-Igoe complex of thirty-three towers. This was classic urban renewal according to Le Corbusier. Unfortunately the towers did not live up to expectations and the whole experiment in social engineering was imploded by the city in 1973.

Louis Sullivan coined the phrase "form follows function" in the early days of the modern movement. Modern architecture was further refined by Ludwig Mies van der Rohe who became the proponent of a type of architecture he described as "less is more." He believed the structure was not as essential in the design, as Le Corbusier taught. In the process, he superimposed his abstract concept on any project regardless of regional tastes and previous traditions.[6] No matter what the building was destined for, Meis divorced it from any previous associations with traditional architecture. In this case, form only follows function in the sense that the need for shelter is fulfilled, not that form follows function with the cultural cues associated with the function. Unfortunately, Meisian austerity leaves no room for the accustomed ornamentation that visually advertises what the function is inside the box. In general, the modernists were strict adherents to a set of principles they believed were universal. Hence, they discounted all previous styles and traditional features, asserting that modern architectural principles were innate. In this respect, adherents of modern architecture are often accused of being extremists, refusing to see value in anything that does not fit their vision.

1. Roth, *Concise History of American Architecture*, 274–332.
2. Venturi, *Complexity and Contradiction in Architecture*, 101–3.
3. Blake, *Form Follows Fiasco*, 15–28.
4. Brolin, *Failure of Modern Architecture*, 88.
5. Gelernter, *History of American Architecture*, 266.
6. Ibid., 267.

Congressional Action for Postwar Armories

In November 1947, the Secretary of Defense appointed a commission of high-ranking civilian and military planners to study the civilian components in the military establishment. The committee chairman was Assistant Secretary of the Army Gordon Gray, and the purpose of the committee was to perform an in-depth review of all the armed services' reserve forces.[7] One of the committee's many concerns was the need for adequate facilities for non–active-duty soldiers. When it came to housing for reserve forces, the military was in a catch-22 situation, similar to that of the interwar years. The federal government was not permitted to use federal money to build armories and reserve training facilities; that responsibility belonged to the states, and the number of armories available for the reserve components was traditionally based on the size of the National Guard force the state felt it needed for internal use. But the post–World War II demand for a larger reserve force meant an increase in the size of the National Guard to numbers over that required by each state. This in turn required more armories than a state needed or wanted to pay for. The problem was who would build them: the states that did not need them or the federal government that did?

The State of Missouri was unprepared to accommodate a National Guard force expansion in 1947. The state had the required population base to fill the federal government's higher quota of forces, but the state fell short of the number of armories that would be required to house a force that was programmed to jump from 4,907 in 1947 to 11,677 as soon as feasible. At the time, Missouri had forty-five armories of all types: state-owned, state-leased, and state-rented. Of those, only twenty-nine were deemed adequate for continued use and sixteen were inadequate, meaning that the facilities lacked sufficient space for equipment storage or they were too small for several units to occupy. Of Missouri's forty-five armories, the state owned only twenty-two; twenty were rented and three were leased.[8] Missouri Guard units were underhoused even before 1940, and the state was unlikely to expend tax revenue in peacetime to accommodate the federal government.

Reorganization of the National Guard on a national scale began in 1946 after the secretary of war decided on a new force number. Adjutant General John A. Harris officially accepted Missouri's allotment of twenty-five units on July 3, 1946.[9] During this process and the accompanying negotiations between the War Department and the states, it was understood that states would be asked to host larger National Guard contingents than they had previously hosted. In fact, the new state quota would be far in excess of the individual state's ability to house them. Since Section 83 of the National Defense Act prohibited the War Department from building National Guard armories, a compromise was needed. As early as 1946, House of Representatives bill 5762 was submitted to change the law to authorize the War Department to appropriate funds for the purchase of land, and for construction and/or expansion of existing armories and support buildings.[10]

By the end of 1950, the National Guard had grown steadily from 353,766 to 369,489. Twenty-seven divisions, twenty regimental combat teams, and twenty-seven air groups allotted nationally in 1946 had been federally recognized. But the dearth of armories, which was acutely short before World War II, became critical with the formation of each authorized unit.[11] A subcommittee of the

---

7.   Gray, *Reserve Forces for National Security*, 1.

8.   Ibid., 179.

9.   National Guard Bureau, *Annual Report … 1946*, 61.

10.   Ibid., 93.

11.   National Guard Bureau, *Annual Report … 1950*, 1.

House Committee on Armed Services convened on March 16 to discuss H.R. 2824, which was the focus of the subcommittee and the subject of testimony by expert witnesses from the military establishment. In his testimony, Secretary of the Army Kenneth Royall made it known that the Army's interest in this legislation was quantitative because the Army had the largest portion of reserve components in the form of National Guard units.[12] Royall was direct in noting the importance of the armory in the Army's plans for recruiting a larger National Guard, but he also noted that inadequate armories, "perhaps most important of all, or certainly of at least as much importance, [had] hurt unit morale as well as general morale among civilian-soldiers and prospective civilian-soldiers."[13] Commenting on armories that did not reflect the Army image, he testified, "Rented quarters are often not appropriate in design. They do not attract men to enlistment or drill. They lend no dignity to the service. Nor do they encourage commanders to assume the onerous tasks of property responsibility, organization, training, recruiting, and leadership."[14] The remedy, according to Royall, was to release rented spaces and where possible replace them with more and better buildings that were state-owned, not leased. Exchanging rented spaces for state-owned spaces could be prohibitively expensive, but Royall asserted that, with proper management and joint utilization of training facilities by Reserve components, a state-owned space could be more cost effective than traditional housing methods.[15]

Of interest in the Secretary of the Army's testimony was his acknowledgement of the importance of building style and its connection to the popular image of the Army. The new armory must "attract men to enlist" and add dignity to the service. Royall also makes a case for a degree of interaction between a local commander who might be more involved in maintenance matters for an appropriate-looking armory building than for a nondescript rented building.

Testifying for the National Guard Bureau, Major General Kenneth F. Cramer itemized the status of state armories across the nation. As of 1948, 4,437 Guard units were housed in 1,969 communities, and the various states had a total of 1,969 armories. Of these only 956 were state-owned; 480 were leased (from a partnership or corporation), and 533 were rented (from an individual). After stating the case for state-owned armories, Bureau Chief Cramer provided a vision of the finished product in the form of "definitive drawings for low-cost, semi-permanent type single-unit and two-unit armories which would provide minimum facilities for classroom, storage and administrative purposes."[16] Cramer stressed the advantage of an armory that served a single unit—location. These proposed armories would be small enough to service communities and areas that did not host a guard unit at that time.[17] Cramer argued that small armories were organizationally and politically attractive because the "strength of the guard, . . . lies in the towns which support a single unit. That is the greater strength of the guard."[18]

At about the same time, in March 1949, a Senate subcommittee heard testimony on a similar bill, S. 960, titled "A Bill to Provide for the Construction, Rehabilitation, Expansion, and Joint

12. US Congress, House, Committee on Armed Services, Subcommittee No. 3, *Hearings on H.R. 2824, . . . and H.R. 4570 . . .*, March 16, 1949, p. 4458.

13. Ibid.

14. Ibid., 4459.

15. Ibid.

16. Ibid., 4526–32.

17. Ibid., 4532.

18. Ibid., 4541.

Utilization of Buildings, Structures, Utilities, and Other Facilities, including the Acquisition of Land, For the Reserve Components of the National Military Establishment of the United States, and for Other Purposes," known as the National Defense Facilities Act of 1949. The Senate bill expanded on the House bill by encompassing all reserve components and limiting the authority of the secretary of defense to influence the location and type of units based in a community. The compromise required the secretary to consult with the state involved before units were removed from an existing community. The Senate bill also reinforced the concept that the new buildings were expected to be interchangeable among all the reserve components.

Despite the importance of this bill to the Department of Defense, the subcommittee testimony did not result in a successful bill in 1949. The secretary of defense dropped his support for the bill and the committee decided to hold it for future action.[19]

In the second session of the Eighty-First Congress, in the spring of 1950, the secretary of defense made the armory bill a top priority. Much of the language remained the same, and the estimated cost of the program was reduced from the original $743 million to $135 million over three years. With new testimony and a celebrity list of supporters, S. 960 was finally voted on by the full Senate in June 1950.[20]

The next session of Congress (Eighty-first Congress, second session) presented another opportunity for the House to pass a new bill, H.R. 8373. The new bill contained much of the previous bill's wording and a provision to authorize a sum not to exceed $400 million, to be used in $50 million increments per fiscal year.

Among the list of experts presenting testimony on this bill was a new entity, the Civilian Components Policy Board of the Office of the Secretary of Defense. Board spokesperson Colonel Alva Fenn testified on behalf of the secretary of defense and covered many of same points Secretary Royall had made the previous year. After Fenn presented his remarks, a committee member asked: "Do you consider the absence of the existence of adequate armories a very serious blow to the morale of the guard and the Reserves?" Colonel Fenn responded, "In my personal opinion, it is the most limiting factor in the Reserve program. It is very difficult to go out and get a fine young man to join any organization and then not have a place for him. He must have a place and he must have a uniform. The place comes first."[21]

Most of the subcommittee testimony to this point dealt with numbers and actions, and occasionally with how the armory would look. In an exchange between Brigadier General E. A. Evans, executive director of the Reserve Officers Association, and Representative W. Sterling Cole (R-NY) of the subcommittee, details of the construction and what was regarded as adequate became clear.

Mr. Cole: I was interested in your view that this money, since it is not enough to go around, to round out the entire program of all the units, should be devoted to nonmonumental structures—I think you used that expression. What type of structure do you have in mind as being nonmonumental?

General Evans: Well, certainly we are not interested in a building that might have a limestone front or might be a high-priced property. We would be perfectly satisfied to have a building somewhat similar to the type of building that the Navy is utilizing or a modification of that. That would be,

19. *Congressional Record* 96 (1950): 8724–26.

20. Ibid.

21. US Congress, House, Committee on Armed Services, Brooks Subcommittee, *Hearings on H.R. 8373*, 6389–91.

perhaps, cinder block construction and a light steel frame rather than a heavy frame of reinforced concrete and a monumental front. In other words, we are interested in a building that can be utilized rather than one that is there for appearance's sake.

Mr. Cole: When you refer to the type used by the Navy, do you also include the Quonset-hut type of structure?

General Evans: "That is correct."[22]

A member of the committee, Overton Brooks (D-LA) noted to General Evans that states had constructed most existing armories without a uniform program to guide them. He wanted to know whether a state that wanted to build a slightly different armory from the standardized plan offered by the Defense Department could do so if the state was willing to pay more than the minimum 25 percent required under this bill. General Evans replied that a state could easily do this since the split of 75 percent to 25 percent was a limit, not a necessary figure to achieve at the cost of all else.[23]

This exchange and other testimony brought out a main theme during the hearings on both the House and Senate bills. The federal government wanted larger troop commitments from the states in order to lower the expense of the regular army, but at the same time, the federal government wanted maximum efficiency in housing to the extent that utility and military requirements dictated the style and look of the new armory. Testimony regarding the importance of the armory as a home of the Guard and how the public and potential recruits perceive it was eventually relegated to secondary importance after cost.

On May 25, 1950, the House Committee on Armed Services met to consider four bills dealing with the armed services. One of these was H.R. 8594, referred to as the Reserve Armory Bill. After remarking on the bill's importance to the reserve system, the committee put the bill up for a floor vote on August 15, 1950.[24] The committee knew that the House version did not match the Senate version, but expected that a conference committee of the House and Senate would settle the differences and the bill would become law.[25] On August 30, 1950, the conference committee issued their report reconciling the House and Senate versions of the National Defense Facilities Act of 1950, and on September 11, 1950, the bill became Public Law 783, which allowed the secretary of defense to contribute funds to state armory projects.[26]

Public Law 783 represented the first time the federal government took a direct role in armory construction, putting the first $16 million to work in 1952. The first contract for a Type 783 armory was approved for the State of Arizona and by 1953, sixty-six new armories were under construction and thirteen were undergoing expansion.[27] The pace after this quickened considerably as each state reached an agreement for cooperation with the federal government. During fiscal years 1952 through 1955, a total of $38.9 million was committed for five hundred projects. The Defense Department issued new space criteria in 1955, allotting 33 percent more area per armory.[28] The

22. Ibid., 6448.

23. Ibid., 6453.

24. US Congress, House, Committee on Armed Services, *Full Committee Hearing on S. 2269, H.R. 8604, S. 2335, H.R. 8594, S.*

25. US Congress, House, Conference Committee, *Conference Report to Accompany H.R. 8594*, 3–6.

26. National Guard Bureau, *Annual Report … 1951*, 18–19.

27. National Guard Bureau, *Annual Report … 1953*, 19–20.

28. National Guard Bureau, *Annual Report … 1955*, 24–25.

State of Alabama anticipated building thirty-two new armories as part of the $38 million construction program in their state alone. Alabama claimed it would have an armory in "every county" of the state built with the 75-to-25-percent funding ratio and each one-unit armory was "planned to be readily adaptable to general community use."[29]

The revised space requirements were an expression of the pace of change in the postwar army. The modern style armories were to be built in greater numbers and the size of each armory would grow. The new demand, unforeseen in 1949, called for more classroom space. In a reversal of armory design since the 1870s, which emphasized large drill hall space for unit maneuvering, the new armories lost drill hall space and gained classrooms as an acknowledgement of the importance of technical training in the modern army. To facilitate armory standardization and keep costs down, the Corps of Engineers commissioned the architectural firm of Reisner and Urbahn of New York to develop the "expansible" armory concept.[30]

Reisner and Urbahn produced three master plans for the expandable armory. Beginning with a base size, the planners envisioned a 400-, 600-, and 1000-man Guard unit. Using the concept of the module, the planners contemplated an armory for a 400-man unit easily converted into a 600-man armory. Using "connecting links," the plan was to add as many additional sections of classrooms and offices as needed for the manpower assigned to the armory.[31] Notable in this plan was the allowance for variation in building material and infrastructure. Depending on where it was to be built, the armory could have a basement or not, it could be of brick, stone, wood, or monolithic cement. In reality, however, there was little room for deviation from the original plan during the first phase of postwar armory construction in 1950. Another twist presented by this plan was the size. In 1949, testimony before the House committee studying H.R. 2824, National Guard Bureau Chief Major General Kenneth F. Cramer stated that the strength of the National Guard was in the small towns and that the small one-unit armory was needed to tap into that strength. But in 1952, planners appear to have abandoned that logic in favor of large metropolitan armories of considerable size.

In 1956, the Eighty-fourth Congress passed Public Law 302, enlarging federal support for the conversion or purchase of new armories. The government would now pay 100 percent of the cost of a purchased or converted armory deemed necessary by the Secretary of the Army to house a reorganized unit. The total amount of government support for armory construction reached $65 million for the years 1952 to 1956, spread over 737 projects.[32] In 1957, the Eighty-fifth Congress passed Public Law 85-215, which continued the federal/state relationship for armory building into the future.[33]

Once the Department of Defense received authority to influence the number and location of state armories, it developed new requirements for armories based on new information. In 1964, the Defense Department conducted a study for future construction and found that, in that year, there were 1,811 adequate armories and another 996 inadequate facilities that required rehabilitation. The new plan proposed to fund 745 replacement armories and 251 alterations and renovation projects at an

29. "New Armories to Have Recreation Use in Alabama."
30. "New-Type Armories are Designed for Expansion."
31. Ibid.
32. National Guard Bureau, *Annual Report ... 1956*, 31–32
33. National Guard Bureau, *Annual Report ... 1958*, 4–5.

estimated cost of $148 million.[34] Twenty years later, the number of all types of armories had increased to 2,851.[35]

Armory construction was now an element of national policy, and this priority with government money propelled the construction of a new type of armory in almost every state. The style of armories built under Public Law 783 and their successors are strikingly similar in Missouri and are commonplace throughout the state. Type 783 armory construction is characterized by a lack of ornamentation, flat roofs, brick walls, and disregard for the importance of visual interpretation.[36] The modern style in armory design (here referred to as the Type 783 style) arose quickly in the post–World War II period but waned by the 1970s. Government mandate is the primary reason the modern style armory is found all across the country.[37] The driving force in Washington was the need to build functional armories quickly and cheaply. The modern armory is a nontraditional variation in the Guard's home history and a perfect reflection of its time.

Once again the federal government, this time based on defense needs and by its own choice, had entered into the armory construction business. The National Guard Bureau standardized plans for buildings and furnished them to interested communities. Under the WPA armory construction program, armories were often built on parcels of land donated by municipalities. This meant that the lots were often small, which limited future expansion and training. In the new armory program, more consideration was given to the site; the suggested lot size was approximately two acres with a street frontage of about 225 feet. Movement in and out of the site was important, so plans called for the site to be accessible from at least one, if not two, paved streets or highways. Preference went to naturally dry and level terrain suitable for building with public sewer and utilities nearby.[38] Unadulterated examples of the Cold War Type 783 style are found in the St. Clair and Jackson Armories.

The first Type 783 armories to be built in Missouri were announced in December 1952. The approximately 12,000-square-foot armories were allotted to the cities of Jackson, Independence, Maryville, and Mexico.[39] Type 783 armories are the zenith of armory standardization: they are rigidly symmetrical, flat-roofed, and rectangular-shaped buildings with a half-story upper level for light and additional height over the drill hall floor. The drill hall is surrounded by U-shaped, flat-roofed, single-story wings, in a floor plan that originated with the WPA/art deco armories of the 1930s. The walls of the wings are blank on the front and rear (although they may have windows on the sides), and the main entry, a double door, is located on the wall recessed between the two ends of the U-shaped wings.

Most of these armories have a brick veneer that varies in color from buff yellow to red brown. Ornamentation is severely limited to metal frame windows, occasionally some enameled brick, and a flagpole placed directly to the side of the structure, usually near the main entrance. Some Cold War armories have partial basements to house heating plants and provide limited storage. Due to their dampness, most basements are not used for those purposes today. Many have rifle ranges, but none are in use today.

34. National Guard Bureau, *Annual Report . . . 1964*, 44–46.
35. National Guard Bureau, *Annual Report . . . 1984*, 3.
36. Gowans, *Styles and Types of North American Architecture*, 273.
37. Ibid., 271.
38. C. H. Engelbrecht to Commander Heavy Mortar Co., Salem, October 7, 1953, Salem Armory folder, MMMH.
39. "Four New Armories to Be Constructed."

The Type 783 style does not include any design elements identifiable with the profession of arms. In fact, without signage, the viewer might mistake any of the buildings for something other than an armory. Modern style armories are testaments to architecture that attempts to be timeless in style by eliminating stylistic elements and capitalizing on simplicity. A modern style building has little ornamentation and no complicated styling that might retard the building process. The activities to take place within the building are secondary to the form of the building as dictated by a design formula.

It is worthwhile to speculate about the impact of modern style armories in small-town America. The Type 783 armories are a product of the modern movement, which found favor in major cities where corporate headquarters and office space bloomed in the postwar era. In rural areas, however, the modern style building was not as widely used. But many Cold War armories are located in small towns because the National Guard had the greatest need in outstate areas. In these more sparsely populated sections of the nation, the stark lines of a Type 783 armory on Main Street or around the town square may be the only example of the modern style to be found in the area. In this respect, the modern style and the art deco/WPA category armories share a common bond: if it were not for the National Guard building programs in the 1930s and 1950s, rural Missouri would not have many examples of either type of architecture. The major difference between the WPA and modern armory is how the buildings have aged. After several decades of use, the latter buildings are among the dingiest, most depressing buildings in the Guard inventory: they have not aged as gracefully as previous armories in different styles.

Had there not been a Cold War, armories in the postwar period may have looked modern but probably not like the cloned versions of modern Type 783 armories scattered around the United States. Patterns in prior armory construction indicate that regional styles and community input typically influenced armories built in each state. If the Cold War had not been a factor, it is probable only a few modern style armories would have been built and those would probably have borrowed stylistic and construction elements from regional traditions. Construction of the substantial number of Type 783 armories in Missouri required a national event on the scale of the Great Depression, in this case the Cold War, to force the government to reenter the armory-building business as the major partner. To make it more politically acceptable, new buildings were required to be open to the general public in a carryover from the Depression-era community center concept. In Missouri alone, federal assistance resulted in thirty-seven new armories, some in towns that had never had a state armory and others constructed as replacements for buildings considered too small.[40]

Type 783 armories have served well as expedients. For the heritage-rich National Guard, however, they are inadequate as symbols of security and strength. It is hard to associate the plain exterior appearance and sterile interior atmosphere of these structures with the Guard mission. Guard members have long made this connection, as noted by a young Guardsman in 1973 commenting on Type 783 armories,

> All of us in the National Guard know the Guard has plenty of advantages, but we also know that the appearance of the average armory is not normally considered one of them. It's a safe bet that no recruiters are using the Guard armories as a big selling point.
>
> We all know what they look like—bland and institutional on the outside—a mixture of OD green and gray on the inside—monuments to concrete and cinder block; practical, functional buildings that

40. National Defense Facilities Act of 1950, Pub. Law 783, in *US Statutes At Large*, 64:829–32.

have served the guard well, but have never won any awards for architectural excellence.[41]

It is ironic that the Guard, the home-based reserve component with allegiance to both state and nation, is partly housed in structures built with more attention paid to speed and cost than to the importance of the organization that calls it home. Critique of the modern style armories is beneficial if only to point out how they do or do not serve the Guard adequately and to provide lessons for future armory styles. Former philosophy professor, university president, social commentator, and architectural critic John Silber has suggested architecture should fulfill three needs: it must be functional, aesthetic, and economic.[42] A building lacking one of the three may be deemed adequate, but Silber states that any style that violates all three qualifies as "architecture of the absurd."[43] It is possible that modern Type 783 armories fall into this "absurd" category. Functionality is well addressed in modern style armories: they provide shelter and security within four walls. But from an occupant's perspective, these armories are not satisfactory functional buildings. For instance, the lighting within many modern drill halls is inadequate, relying too much on the ribbon windows over the drill hall. The flexibility built into the basic design and seen as a hallmark of the type is overstated. The basements (when included) tend to be wet, and the interior walls and floors are sterile. Without a great deal of additional thought to soften the edges of the basic walls, the functional aspect of the interior overshadows other human wants that lead to occupant contentment.

The aesthetics of the style as intended by the designers is minimal, leaving much to be desired for a uniformed service. The entrance is unobtrusive, often nothing more than a doorway along the front façade, when it should be a complementing and inviting feature. The exterior is also void of interest from the flat roof to the brick color that tends to look dull or discolored over time. Lack of landscaping around the buildings only emphasizes the austerity of the building. But the major drawback of the building's appearance is the total lack of any identification with the National Guard. Its function is ambiguous: is it a warehouse? a jail? a factory?[44] Few would guess on first viewing the Type 783 building that it is a National Guard armory.

Out of the three criteria, the only area where Type 783 armories may succeed is the economic factor. These are inexpensive buildings, but they often do not meet the economic threshold of success when one factors in maintenance costs. Wet basements below are mirrored with leaking roofs above, and repetitive repair work eliminates the cost advantage of the initial construction savings.

Type 783 armories served their purpose and confirmed the utility of the interior arrangement. In addition, they inadvertently confirm the importance of visual appeal to a Guard Armory. An uninviting armory runs counter to the Guard's image. Lessons learned in this category contributed to the next generation of armory construction exhibiting far more exterior appeal.

41. Walker, "Missouri Guard Acquires New Armory."
42. Silber, *Architecture of the Absurd*, 15.
43. Ibid, 91.
44. Todd, *New York's Historic Armories*, 271.

Inventory of Type 783 Armories (by date built)

Fig. 5.1: 135th Rear Operations Center Armory, 2010
4350 South Kingshighway Boulevard, St. Louis
Style: modern
Built 1947–1948; occupied 2007–present
Architect/builder unknown
Photo: Grant L. Day

Fig. 5.2: 1140th Engineer Battalion Armory, 1998
224 West Park Street, Jackson, Cape Girardeau County
Style: Type 783
Built 1953; occupied 1954–present
Architect/builder: Prichard and Associates
Photo: Chuck MacFall

Fig. 5.3: Martin-Pedersen Armory, 1998

709 College Park Drive, Maryville, Nodaway County

Style: Type 783

Built 1953; occupied 1955–2003 (currently used by Northwest Missouri State University)

Architect/builder: Prichard and Associates

Photo: Chuck MacFall

Fig. 5.4: 1175th Military Police Company Armory, 1998

310 East McKinsey, Moberly, Randolph County

Style: Modified Type 783

Built 1954; occupied 1954–present

Architect/builder: Prichard and Associates

Photo: Wiegers

Fig. 5.5: Battery C, 128th Field Artillery Armory, 1998
475 South Davis, Marshall, Saline County
Style: Type 783
Built 1955; occupied 1956–present
Architect/builder: Prichard and Associates
Photo: Wiegers

Fig. 5.5a: New exterior of Marshall armory, 2002 (Photo: Wiegers)

Fig. 5.6: Company A, 203rd Engineer Battalion Armory, 1998
710 Anderson Street, Anderson, McDonald County
Style: Type 783
Built 1955; occupied 1956–present
Architect/builder: Prichard and Associates
Photo: Wiegers

Fig. 5.7: Harry S. Truman Armory, 1998
2323 South Crysler, Independence, Jackson County
Style: Type 783
Built 1955; occupied 1956–present
Architect/builder: Prichard and Associates
Photo: Chuck MacFall

Fig. 5.8: Kenneth L. Bradford Memorial Armory, 1998
917 West Curtis Street, Mexico, Audrain County
Style: Type 783
Built 1955; occupied 1955–present
Architect/builder unknown
Photo: Wiegers

Fig. 5.9: Company B, 203rd Engineer Armory, 1998
1800 Richard Webster Drive, Carthage, Jasper County
Style: Type 783 variant
Built 1956; occupied 1957–present
Architect/builder: M-P Construction Co.
Photo: MMMH

The Carthage Armory is typical of Type 783 armories except for the exterior covered in Carthage marble instead of brick. The armory was built in 1956, inspected by Missouri Adjutant General A. D. Sheppard in March 1957, and dedicated on June 8, 1957. It is one of the earliest modern style armories to be completed in Missouri.

The National Guard has been in Carthage since 1876. Various units had rented space on Howard Street south of the Drake Hotel[45] and the headquarters of the 135th Infantry rented rooms north of the square on Main Street because some in the community felt rented armories were adequate and were

45. "February 7 Is Target Date for New Armory Bids," *Carthage Evening Press,* January 10, 1956.

not interested in participating in the 1935 WPA program for armory construction.[46] The Missouri adjutant general held a public meeting in Carthage to promote community involvement in the WPA armory program but received more negative than positive responses. One citizen, H. W. Putnam, owner of the Putnam Lumber Company in Carthage, wrote, "I certainly enjoyed the little visit I had with you the other day and trust that the Armory in Carthage will not be built. As I told you, we rent the Armory here to the National Guard."[47]

Captain Stanley E. Bye of Carthage reported to the adjutant general in November 1935 that the community was only in favor of the armory if the state sponsored it and paid for it. The Carthage Chamber of Commerce was prepared to donate nine and a half acres on the condition that the state allocate money for the local share of the construction costs. Bye noted that if no armory were built, "Pacifists and pinks and some of the owners of buildings upon which the state is now paying rent will be well satisfied."[48] With no local support for participating in the WPA armory-building program, Carthage would wait over twenty years for a state-owned armory.

Because the 1957 armory was to include both a headquarters staff and a Guard unit, the building, at 18,620 square feet, exceeded the square footage for a one-unit armory (12,112 square feet). Aside from its setting in a city park, the distinguishing feature of this modern style armory is the exterior treatment. Instead of the typical dull yellow to red/brown brick, this armory is faced with Carthage stone. When the armory project was approved, the mayor of Carthage wrote the adjutant general of Missouri asking if locally quarried Carthage gray marble could be used instead of brick.[49] Adjutant General Sheppard agreed to this change as long as the stone cost no more than the lowest bid for brick.[50] The armory cost $161,802, of which the federal government paid 75 percent.

Fig. 5.10: Company B, 1140th Engineer Battalion Armory, 1998
905 South Kingshighway Boulevard, Perryville, Perry County
Style: Type 783
Built 1956; occupied 1958–present
Architect: Prichard and Associates / Builder: Kiefner Construction Company
Photo: Chuck MacFall

46. "Armory Bids Approved," *Carthage Evening Press*, April 10, 1956.

47. H. W. Putnam to Harold W. Brown, October 18, 1935, Armory correspondence files, MMMH.

48. Stanley E. Bye to A. D. Sheppard, November 17, 1935, Armory correspondence files, MMMH.

49. Glenn C. Joyce to A. D. Sheppard, May 25, 1955, Armory correspondence files, MMMH.

50. A. D. Sheppard to Glenn Joyce, June 3, 1955, Armory correspondence files, MMMH.

Fig. 5.11: Company A, 735th Support Battalion Armory, 1997
106 Broadway, Lamar, Barton County
Style: Type 783
Built 1956; occupied 1957–present
Architect/builder unknown
Photo: Wiegers

Lamar, Missouri, is notable for the number of World War II admirals and politicians that hail from the small town. This includes a president, Harry S. Truman, and US Navy Admirals Charles A. Lockwood, Freeland A. Daubin, and Thomas S. Combs.[51] The Lamar armory was constructed in 1958 using $112,500 in federal funds. The Lamar Chamber of Commerce sold the land for the armory to the state for one dollar on October 23, 1954. The building received a new roof in 2006, but otherwise has remained unaltered.

Fig. 5.11a: New roof on the Lamar armory, 2006 (Photo: Chuck MacFall)

51. Meyer, *Heritage of Missouri*, 683.

Fig. 5.12: Camden Bock Armory, 1997
400 West 10th Street, Portageville, New Madrid County
Style: Type 783
Built 1956; occupied 1957–present
Architect: Prichard and Associates / Builder: Jos. T. Stryker and Associates
Photo: Wiegers

Fig. 5.13: St. Clair Armory, 1997
375 Commercial Avenue, St. Clair, Franklin County
Style: Type 783
Built 1956; occupied 1957–present
Architect/builder: Prichard and Associates
Photo: Wiegers

Fig. 5.14: Headquarters and Headquarters Company, 135th Engineer Battalion Armory, ca. 1960

2626 Independence Drive, Cape Girardeau, Cape Girardeau County

Style: Type 783

Built 1957; occupied 1958–present

Architect/builder: Prichard and Associates

Photo: MMMH

In 1957, a new Cape Girardeau Armory replaced the art deco/WPA style building that became the Brase Community Center. National Guard reorganization after World War II resulted in the old armory being considered too small for the larger planned unit. The City of Cape Girardeau sold a lot of 4.62 acres for the new armory to the state for one dollar.[52] The estimated cost to build this armory was $185,000, of which the federal government paid $137,750 and the state paid $47,240. The armory was built using the standard floor plan with additional space for headquarters staff. The basement contains a rifle range and exits to a parking lot. When this armory was constructed, the surrounding area was rural. In the years since construction, the surrounding area has been highly developed and a busy highway now cuts directly across the armory frontage.

Fig. 5.15: Headquarters, 135th Aviation Battalion Armory, 1986

343 East Gay Street, Warrensburg, Johnson County

Style: Type 783

Built 1957; occupied 1958–present

Architect/builder: Gastinger and Walker Associates

Photo: Chuck MacFall

52. Warranty Deed from City of Cape Girardeau to State of Missouri, November 24, 1952, Cape Girardeau folder, MNGFE.

An unforeseen fire in the Warrensburg WPA armory spurred the planning and construction of the current modern style armory. On November 10, 1954, the WPA armory on Holden Street burned, leaving only charred masonry and stone walls where the 90-by-150-foot armory once stood.[53] The WPA armory and its replacement building were products of enthusiastic support from the community of Warrensburg. On August 22, 1955, the City of Warrensburg sold the Guard a plot of land on East Gay Street for one dollar.[54] The new armory was built in 1958 based on plans by architects Gastinger and Walker and is home to Headquarters Company, Thirty-fifth Division and to Headquarters and Service Company, 135th Aviation Battalion.

Since the 1940s, the armory and unit have been associated with aviation activities of some type. A local airfield was used for a short time by small Guard planes, but nearby Whiteman Air Force Base is now a focal point of activity. In 1986, the unit was reorganized and redesignated the 635th Attack Helicopter Battalion. The unit remained on Gay Street until it moved to a new armory on Whiteman Air Force Base in 1997.

Fig. 5.16: Company A, 735th Supply Battalion Armory, 1997
1400 West Cherry, Nevada, Vernon County
Style: Type 783
Built 1957; occupied 1958–present
Architect: Prichard and Associates / Builder: T. J. Longabaugh Construction Co.
Photo: Wiegers

Fig. 5.16a: New roof on the Nevada armory, 1998 (Photo: Wiegers)

53. C. H. Engelbrecht to Chief, National Guard Bureau, January 31, 1955, Armory correspondence files, MMMH.

54. Warranty Deed, City of Warrensburg to State of Missouri, August 22, 1955, Warrensburg folder, MNGFE.

Fig. 5.17: "Big Blue" Armory/2175th Military Police Armory, 1997
801 Armory Drive, Jefferson City, Cole County
Style: Modified Type 783
Built 1958; occupied 1959–present
Architect/builder: Prichard and Associates
Enlarged 1987; Architect/builder: JCA & Associates
Photo: MMMH (original configuration)

The Jefferson City armory is perhaps the most eye-catching armory in the whole state. Perched atop a bluff at one end of the Jefferson City/Missouri River bridge, the armory is often referred to as "Big Blue" for the obvious reason: it is clad in a dark blue metal skin. This armory building reflects two stages of construction. The original building used the common U-shape plan around a central drill hall. In 1987, the building was expanded and covered in vertical-seamed metal sheets that were wrapped around and over the original façade.

When Mayor Arthur W. Ellis and Missouri Adjutant General A. D. Sheppard turned the first spades of earth at a groundbreaking ceremony for the new armory on May 10, 1957,[55] the community and the National Guard had already been working on the project for nine years. After seven years of planning, searching for a site, and raising money, the city transferred a plot of land to the state in June 1954 to build an armory that was supposed to be a scaled-down version of the Pentagon in Washington but with a flat back.[56] In early 1955, the ground at the new armory site was leveled off; however, it would take two more years to resolve problems involving utilities and road access before the groundbreaking ceremony could take place.[57] By December 1955, Jefferson City's armory had moved to second place, behind the Salem armory, on the list of armories to be built.[58] In January 1957, the Army released $180,000 for the construction of the new armory in Jefferson City and announced that the new armory would house a unit of 265 men.[59] On April 9, 1957, the city announced that Joseph T. Stryker and Associates of Portageville, Missouri, had submitted the lowest construction bid of $183,919. The total cost of the armory was estimated to be $238,496;[60] it eventually cost $263,763.85.[61] Construction on the new 22,000-square-foot armory was completed in 1958.

55. "Mayor Breaks Ground in Ceremony," *Daily Capital News*, May 11, 1957.

56. Ibid.

57. "Say Local Armory Site Will be Ready," *Daily Capital News*, May 1, 1955.

58. "City Could Get Armory in Next Fiscal Year," *Daily Capital News*, December 31, 1955.

59. "Money for 106 Armories," *Carthage Evening Press*, January 19, 1957.

60. "Say Local Armory Site Will be Ready," *Daily Capital News*, May 1, 1955.

61. "Jefferson City Armory Dedication Program," September 13, 1958, Jefferson City folder, MMMH.

In 1986, the National Guard planned to reactivate the Thirty-fifth Infantry Division (Mech.), so an alteration was necessary for additional space. Bids for the new project were opened on August 7, 1989, and Ludwig and Associates of Jefferson City were awarded the construction contract. The architect for the 27,000-square-foot addition was JCA and Associates of Jefferson City. The federal government was to pay $1,107,464, while Missouri was to provide the other $25,000. The total cost of the additional project was to be nearly $1,132,464.[62] Construction on the project was completed in 1987.

The interesting dark-blue siding on the armory was chosen, according to some, from color samples viewed in bad lighting; others claim it was simply the cheapest siding available. It turns out that the siding color was the choice of the architect. The Missouri Guard facility personnel reluctantly agreed to the color, which gave the building its current nickname of "Big Blue."[63]

Fig. 5.17a: Jefferson City Armory after addition, 1998 (Photo: Chuck MacFall)

62. Paul L. Junkans, "Information Paper," September 12, 1986, Lexington folder, MNGFE.

63. Ibid.

Fig. 5.18: French-Taggart Memorial Armory, 1998
810 South Marigold, Clinton, Henry County
Style: Type 783
Built 1958; occupied 1959–present
Architect: Prichard and Associates / Builder: A. J. Seivers Construction
Photo: Chuck MacFall

In 1935, the City of Clinton was one of many small communities struggling with the Depression and a small tax base. When the WPA armory plan was presented to the city council, it was a case of poor timing combined with a lack of will. According to Clinton Mayor Floyd Sperry, the city had just recently committed all available city revenue to sewer and park projects and did not have funds remaining to contribute to a new armory.[64] Hence, Clinton did not get an armory until the post–World War II years.

The City of Clinton did not miss its second opportunity to acquire an armory building. It sold land for an armory to the State of Missouri for one dollar on February 8, 1955. Almost two years later, the Army released funds totaling approximately $112,500 for construction of the 105-man armory to house Company E Second Medium Tank Battalion (Patton) 203rd Armor.[65] On June 7, 1959, the new 16,280-square-foot armory was dedicated as the French-Taggart Memorial Amory, named for two Guard members killed in World War II.[66]

Fig. 5.19: 175th Military Police Battalion Armory, 1997
1501 Westminster, Fulton, Callaway County
Style: Type 783 gable variant
Built 1959; occupied 1960–present

64. Floyd Sperry to Harry H. Tooley, October 4, 1935, Armory correspondence files, MMMH.
65. "Money for 106 Armories," *Carthage Evening Press*, January 19, 1957.
66. Company "E" 2nd Medium Tank Battalion (Patton), 203rd Armor, "Dedication Program," June 7, 1959, Clinton folder, MMMH.

Architect: Butler and Associates / Builder: Shell Construction

Photo: Wiegers

This armory is similar in plan to most modern armories; however, this building has a distinctive triple-gable roof. This building is the fourth armory in Fulton since 1940. With most rented armories, termination of a lease often leaves little time for preparation. In 1957, the National Guard was leasing the basement of McKee Hall on the Missouri School for the Deaf campus. In March of that year, school superintendent Lloyd A. Harrison terminated the lease with sixty days notice to make room for a campus building project.[67] Plans for a permanent home were soon in the making. The Callaway County Fair Association transferred title to approximately five acres in two deeds, one dated June 30, 1954, and another dated June 4, 1959, to encourage construction. According to the local newspaper's estimate, the one-unit armory would cost $77,000.[68]

Fig. 5.20: Detachment 1, 1438th Engineer Company Armory, 1998

1201 West Rolla Street, Salem, Dent County

Style: Type 783

Built 1959; occupied 1960–present

Architect/builder: James T. Roberts

Photo: Chuck MacFall

Basic agreement for construction of the Salem National Guard Armory came on August 24, 1955.[69] Nearly two years later, in March 1957, the City of Salem found a suitable location for the armory and on March 26, 1957, James A. and Agnes Pines sold the land to the state for one dollar.[70] In January 1957, the Army released the funds for the construction of the armory. Salem was authorized to spend $112,500 to build an armory to house 143 men.[71] James T. Roberts Sr., a general contractor from Houston, Missouri, was the successful bidder for the Salem Armory at $167,489.[72]

67. Lloyd A. Harrison to A. D. Sheppard, March 27, 1957, Armory correspondence files, MMMH.

68. "Reserve Armory Contract to Be Let During Fiscal Period," *Fulton Daily Sun-Gazette*, January 4, 1957.

69. C. H. Engelbrecht to Chief, National Guard Bureau, January 31, 1955, Armory correspondence files, MMMH.

70. General Warranty Deed from James A. Pines and Agnes Pines to the State of Missouri, March 26, 1957, Salem folder, MNGFE.

71. "Money for 106 Armories," *Carthage Evening Press*, January 19, 1957.

72. "City Armory Bids $238,496," *Daily Capital News*, April 19, 1957.

Fig. 5.21: Harry E. Gladish Memorial Armory, 1997
408 South 26th Street, Lexington, Lafayette County
Style: Type 785 gable variant
Built 1960; enlarged 1987; occupied 1960–present
Architect: McCoy, Hutchinson, & Stone / Builder: Butler and Associates
Photo: Wiegers

This armory is memorable for the distinct triple-gable roofline, similar to that of the armory in Fulton. The City of Lexington received its new 15,958-square-foot National Guard Armory in 1960, and the building dedication was held on November 6, 1960. Thirty years later, however, the armory proved to be too small when additional units—the Thirty-fifth Infantry Division DISCOM (Division Support Command) and Company C, 110th Engineer Battalion—were added. The 219 additional personnel required an expansion of 17,005 square feet on the east side of the original structure in 1987. This alteration to the building and the addition of another 3,612 square feet to the 1960 building created a 36,575-square-foot armory.[73]

The architectural firm of McCoy, Hutchinson, and Stone Architects of Kansas City, Missouri, designed the new addition and Irvinbilt Construction Company of Chillicothe, Missouri, submitted the winning bid. The final cost of the new addition was estimated at $851,000, of which the federal government was responsible for $833,750 and the State of Missouri provided $17,250.[74] At the groundbreaking ceremony for the new addition on October 4, 1987, the building was rededicated as the Harry E. Gladish Memorial Armory, as requested by Congressman Ike Skelton.[75]

Fig. 5.21a: Interior of Lexington armory, 1998 (Photo: Chuck MacFall)

73. Paul L. Junkans, "Information Paper," September 12, 1986, Lexington folder, MNGFE.
74. Ibid.
75. Paul L. Junkans to Division of Design and Construction, April 13, 1988, Lexington folder, MNGFE.

Fig. 5.22: Company D, 1140th Engineer Battalion Armory, 1998
1210 Morris Street, Farmington, St. Francois County
Style: Type 783
Built 1960; occupied 1961–present
Architect/builder: Bruce Barnes
Photo: Wiegers

The Farmington armory is one of several in the state to be fitted with a new steel roof that covers the original flat roof over the drill hall.

Fig. 5.23: Mel Carnahan Memorial Armory, 1997
201 Fairground Road, Rolla, Phelps County
Style: Type 783
Built 1962; occupied 1963–present
Architect/builder: Prichard and Associates
Photo: Chuck MacFall

The armory in Rolla was the only armory in the state constructed to share its building. Half of the building was occupied by the Rolla Army Reserve Center until 2010, when the Jefferson Barracks Armory was completed as a "joint use" facility with the Army Reserve. Constructed in 1963, the armory was unnamed until 2000 when it was christened the Mel Carnahan Memorial Armory in honor of the sitting governor after he was killed in a plane accident. The overall complex is called the Armed Forces Reserve Center.

On April 11, 1960, the National Guard purchased the necessary land for a new armory from the Rolla Chamber of Commerce. However, due to some wording difficulties in the deed, the State of Missouri and the National Guard were unable to finalize plans for construction.[76] On December 28, 1961, approval for the construction of the armory arrived and the building contract was awarded to Prichard Construction of Independence, Missouri.[77]

76. Warranty Deed by Corporation, City of Rolla, April 11, 1960, Rolla folder, MMMH.

77. William B. Blatt to Adjutant General, State of Missouri, December 28, 1961, Armory correspondence files, MMMH.

Fig. 5.24: Detachment 1, Company D, 1140th Engineer Battalion Armory, 1997
104 Armory Street, Fredericktown, Madison County
Style: Type 783
Built 1963; occupied 1963–present
Architect/builder: Bruce Barnes
Photo: Chuck MacFall

Fig. 5.25: Service Battery, 129th Field Artillery Armory, 1998
860 East Lexington, Richmond, Ray County
Style: Type 783
Built 1963; occupied 1964–present
Architect/builder: Prichard and Associates
Photo: Chuck MacFall

Fig. 5.26: Company E, 735th Support Battalion Armory, 1998
1 Armory Drive, Warrenton, Warren County
Style: Type 783
Built 1963; occupied 1964–present
Architect/builder: Bruce Barnes
Photo: Chuck MacFall

Fig. 5.27: Detachment 1, 203rd Engineer Battalion Armory, 1997
600 South Ellis, Webb City, Jasper County
Style: Type 783
Built 1964; occupied 1965–1997 (currently Regional Technical Education Center)
Architect/builder: Southwest Engineering Company
Photo: Chuck MacFall

Fig. 5.28: William E. "Bub" Lewis Armory, 1997
1555 Veterans Drive, DeSoto, Jefferson County
Style: Type 783
Built 1965; occupied 1965–present
Architect/builder: Bruce Barnes
Photo: Chuck MacFall

This armory has been altered over the years with a new brick exterior and several roof treatments ending with a hipped roof over the original flat design.

Fig. 5.29: Former Office of the Adjutant General and Emergency Operation Center, 1997

1717 Industrial Drive, Jefferson City, Cole County

Style: international

Built ca. 1968; occupied 1968–1993

Architect/builder: Ralph Oberlechner

Photo: Chuck MacFall

After the National Guard Headquarters left temporary offices in the state capitol building, it took up residence in a building constructed to fit its needs in the 1960s. The 1717 Industrial Drive building has four floors above ground for the adjutant general and staff, and several floors below ground for the State Emergency Management Agency. The building was constructed of concrete with a brick-veneer first floor entrance, to enable it to withstand a major attack and leave the emergency office in the below-ground level untouched. Although centrally located in Jefferson City, the headquarters building had certain limitations, such as very little space for vehicle and equipment storage and maintenance, and general urban development that negated any chance of future expansion. The Missouri Guard stayed in this location for twenty-five years until a larger and more spacious complex was completed in 1993. Presently the facility is under the Missouri Department of Corrections and houses the Missouri Vocational Enterprises.

Fig. 5.30: 110th Engineer Battalion Armory, 1998
7600 Ozark Road, Kansas City, Jackson County
Style: Modified Type 783
Built 1973; occupied 1974–present
Architect: Angus McCullum and Associates / Builder: D. F. Cahill Construction Co.
Photo: Chuck MacFall

Fig. 5.31: 1137th Military Police Company Armory, 1997
1450 North Bypass, Kennett, Dunklin County
Style: Modified Type 783
Built 1985; occupied 1986–present
Architect: Donnellar and Associates / Builder: Huffman Construction
Photo: Chuck MacFall

Fig. 5.32: Company G, 135th Aviation Armory, 1998
1076 Highland Street, Aurora, Lawrence County
Style: Modified Type 783
Built 1991; occupied 1992–present
Architect/builder: Sides Construction Co.
Photo: Chuck MacFall

Chapter 6
Traditional Revival Armories
The Postmodern Category

The strict dogma of the modern style and negative public reactions to the designs of inferior imitators inspired another change in architectural style.[1] In the three-quarters of a century since the modern style appeared and roughly twenty-five years since the end of World War II, American culture moved from the idea of design theory being dominated by utilitarian progress to a design theory that incorporated both progress and traditional designs. Robert Venturi, a postmodern architect famous for celebrating the complexities of vernacular architecture, playfully satirized modern architect Mies van der Rohe's famous line "less is more" when he wrote "less is a bore."[2]

Postmodern architecture picked up steam in the 1970s and incorporated many qualities that were anathema to modern architecture, such as complexity and subjectivity meant to replace modernism's stricture and selectivity. In a supreme irony, the attempt to eliminate symbols in modern designs unintentionally forced modern architects to invent the equivalent of their own substitute ornamentation.[3] Postmodern designers also objected to the extravagant claim that the modern building was a universal form applicable to all cultures. In contrast, the postmodern architects proposed to focus on the individual person and local culture, and in this way emphasized the connection between the building and the environment. Postmodern architecture is intended to be interpreted by the viewer, and out of that interpretation comes the building's reality, rather than having the reality spelled out in four blank walls. In some variants of modern architecture there exists a level of high- and low-culture buildings, but in postmodern building, the distinction between high and low has been blurred so that "anything goes with anything."[4]

In the 1970s, the severity of the modern armory style began to weaken as architects were again incorporating elements of style, color, and mixed materials in new armory construction. The traditional revival style armory resulted after a period of transition beginning with armories, such as the Joplin armory (fig. 6.2), that look modern but share attributes with the postmodern category, instead of a dramatic pronouncement as occurred with Type 783 armories.

In 1984 the US Army Reserve completed a *Design Guide for U. S. Army Reserve Facilities*. After years of building modern facilities, the Army Reserve decided to refine the modern style by allowing architectural nuances that improved a building's overall image. Among the expectations for

1. Aaltonen, *History of Architecture*, 22.

2. Venturi, *Complexity and Contradiction in Architecture*, 17.

3. Ibid, 139.

4. Callinicos, *Against Post-Modernism*, 12.

future construction was the increased use of shapes and symbols connected with Army history. The *Design Guide* goal of an "aesthetically pleasing building" was put on a par with highly touted goals of functionality and energy efficiency in Reserve facilities.[5] The *Guide* indicates that federal agencies were aware of a change in architecture theory by the 1980s.

In August 1986, the General Accounting Office (GAO) responded to a series of questions from the US Senate about the role for the National Guard in national defense, the condition of armories to fulfill the Guard mission, and the degree of participation of the states in building armories with the 75-to-25-percent program. The GAO report assessed the current inventory of armories. Those over twenty-five years old were suspect on several accounts. First, armory designs in 1935 or 1950 assumed a need for a space of 10,000 square feet or smaller, but the armory in 1980 required 20,000 square feet. In 1938, the National Guard Bureau was satisfied with 2.57 acres of land, but in 1980 the bureau was asking for ten acres or more.[6]

The GAO found that, starting in 1950, the enlarged Guard was housing more full-time personnel. Office space had to be provided for these personnel, to the detriment of space for training. In addition, portions of the drill floor and some classroom space were converted to storage for all types of small and large equipment.[7] Many older armories used every available nook and cranny of the building for office space, often at the expense of equipment storage. This need presented the visitor with an unsightly interior cluttered with makeshift offices.

A concern for planners in the 1980s was the maintenance condition of the Army National Guard's 2,755 state-owned armories. By one estimate, the lack of repair and regular maintenance of state facilities had built up to a backlog of maintenance and repairs that would cost $172 million.[8] Until the mid-1980s, the states were responsible for all maintenance at state and federal/state armories. The federal government paid little for maintenance and the states, Missouri included, paid scant attention to paying for regular maintenance—the very situation the GAO report deplored.

The Missouri National Guard Headquarters staff foresaw support building in Congress for reform, and anticipating the GAO findings, started to push for increased funding. In 1985, the State of Missouri passed a $600 million bond issue for improvements to state buildings and property.[9] One result of this state largesse was eight new armories in Missouri (Aurora, Boonville, Festus, Fulton, Harrisonville, Kennett, Monett, and St. Joseph) and expansions to three existing armories (Jefferson City/Big Blue, Lexington, and Springfield).[10] The newest armories have carried the community center and joint use concepts to a new level of cooperation between local municipalities and the Guard. In Maryville, Dexter, and Sedalia, the communities joined with the Guard to add a separate wing to the armory as community space. The cities have access to the armory facilities when training is not in progress, as before, as well as their own civic center areas.

The City of Maryville assisted the Guard in finding a new site to build on. Instead of settling for the use of the new armory, the city decided to construct a new community center, owned by the city but connected to the new armory. In the new configuration, the community center has access to

5. McCormick, *Design Guide for US Army Reserve Facilities*, 4.

6. Zorinsky, *Army National Guard: Opportunities to Improve the Condition and Operation of Armories*, 3.

7. Ibid., 20–21.

8. Ibid., 25–27.

9. SB 187, in *Laws of the State of Missouri, 1985*, 432–53.

10. Paul L. Junkans to Robert Wiegers, personal communication, June 12, 2007.

joint use areas such as the drill hall, kitchen, and classrooms. The cooperative spirit allowed a larger building to be built than either party could afford.

Postmodern armories reflect a return to customary style elements starkly missing in the modern style armories. In contrast to the modern style armories, traditional revival armories display peaked and gabled roofs, asymmetrical window arrangements, formal main entrances, and multiple types of construction materials, resulting in modern yet aesthetically pleasing buildings. Internally, the drill hall floor follows the standard pattern for postwar armories of a rectangular drill hall with offices and training rooms on three sides. Very large armories vary from this pattern with more space allotted for offices. Basements, full or partial, and theater stages centered on the drill hall, both common in earlier periods, are no longer present.

A classic example of the traditional revival style is the Festus armory (fig. 6.7), built in 1991. A two-story pillar flanked by glass doors and transoms dominates the two-story front façade. To accentuate the width of the entrance, the same color of the pillar continues to each side of the entryway until it ends in a series of descending squares to the first-floor level. This building has an entrance that is centered and an overall appeal that is modern with traditional architectural elements.

The Harrisonville armory (built 1988; fig. 6.5) is a combination of four large areas of glass with two wide vertical bands of color that give its small façade distinction. The main entrance is offset to one side of the structure with a set of doors that repeat the color of the four massive window areas. Attention is drawn to the entry by a concrete column, flagpole, and black sloping roofline.

The Boonville armory (built 1990; fig. 6.6) is a very successful traditional revival building. It incorporates a sloping roofline that joins a second-story vertical glass wall topped by a gabled metal roof. Few vent and utility pipes clutter the clean roofline, which is clearly visible as the armory is approached. The sloping eaves extend out to join with the exterior wall, and square windows interrupt the brown and beige horizontal bands of brick accentuated by double rows of glass blocks.

Traditional revival architecture rejects the prescribed forms of the modern style by returning to several traditional styles, often in one building. Because reality is open to interpretation, postmodern architecture is easily viewed as confusing, irreverent, or fun. What makes postmodern different today might be called the march of time, when those aspects of the modern movement that were meant to be avant-garde are not as awe-inspiring or inflammatory any longer, that which was modern is now passé. Some architects believe a new trend in architecture is already underway, supplanting the accepted idea of what constitutes postmodern, unimaginatively termed for the present "neo-modern." Supposedly a continuation of the real modern philosophy without the baggage of unnecessary assertions about universality and strict interpretation, neo-modern architecture strives to eliminate the formal rules of modern architecture in favor of something new. For instance, neo-modernists would not follow Le Corbusier and level the old city, but would fight to save those parts that are worthy of standing beside the new creation.

Inventory of Traditional Revival Armories (by date built)

Fig. 6.1: Major General Ralph E. Truman Memorial Armory, 1990
1400 North Freemont, Springfield, Greene County
Style: traditional modified
Built 1962; modified 1986, 1989; occupied 1963–present
Architect/builder: Wayne D. Johnson
Photo: MMMH

Fig. 6.2: 203rd Engineer Battalion Armory, 1997
2000 West 32nd Street, Joplin, Jasper County
Style: traditional revival
Built 1974; occupied 1975–present
Architect: Ralph Oberlechner and Associates / Builder: M-P Construction Company
Photo: Wiegers

Fig. 6.3: Command Sergeant Major Erby Chase Memorial Armory, 2002
561 Highway 61 South, Hannibal, Marion County
Style: traditional revival
Built 1974; occupied 1977–present
Architect: Eugene J. Mackey III, Inc. / Builder: Bleigh Construction
Photo: Chuck MacFall

The Hannibal armory is an early example of the traditional revival style. Unique to this armory is the position of the vehicle entrance to the drill floor, situated at a right angle to the main entrance doors. This vehicle access is necessitated by the hilltop orientation of the armory. The Hannibal armory is located on the site of the old Hannibal State Dairy Farm, now part of the Huckleberry City Park. It replaced the often-flooded Admiral Coontz Armory in downtown Hannibal. The city sold the approximately six-acre site to the state for one dollar on December 12, 1973.[11] As in many cases, the sale was on condition that an armory be built on site or the land would revert to the city. Construction of the $620,000 armory began on June 12, 1974, and was completed in December 1976. It was dedicated as the Command Sergeant Major Erby Hilton Chase Memorial Armory on May 7, 1977.

Fig. 6.4: Mayes Memorial Armory, 1997
301 North Woodbine, St. Joseph, Buchanan County
Style: traditional revival
Built 1986–88; occupied 1988–present
Architect: Cooper, Carlson, Duy, and Ritchie / Builder: Grace Construction
Photo: Chuck MacFall

The large armory in St. Joseph incorporates aspects of the modern and traditional revival styles. In order to keep a long-established Signal Corps company in St. Joseph, the city and Guard began as early

11. Deed, City of Hannibal to State of Missouri, December 12, 1973, Marion County, Book 533, Page 3087, Hannibal folder, MNGFE.

as 1979 to plan a new building. By 1984, the armory at 9th and Monterey Streets was too small for the number of trucks and vehicles assigned to the unit, many of which were stored at Rosecrans Air Guard Base. The unit needed a bigger facility.

The Woodbine armory site was part of the State Mental Hospital #2 and a working dairy farm. It closed in the 1960s and fifteen acres of the site were acquired by the Missouri Guard from Missouri Western University.[12] On September 27, 1986, groundbreaking ceremonies were held for the new armory. The St. Joseph Armory was completed in 1988 by W. M. Grace Construction on a design by architects Cooper, Carlson, Duy, and Ritchie. The new armory has a rifle range, a kitchen, offices, lockers, classrooms, and an organizational and maintenance shop with ample parking. The project cost was $2.2 million and the armory was dedicated in April of 1988 as the Mayes Memorial Armory after a long-time member and supporter of the unit.

Fig. 6.5: 1139th Military Police Company Armory, 1997
1503 South Jefferson Parkway, Harrisonville, Cass County
Style: traditional revival
Built 1987; occupied 1988–present
Architect: Gastinger, Rees, Walker / Builder: Irvinbilt Construction Co.
Photo: Chuck MacFall

The Harrisonville armory clearly shows the break from modern style with a new emphasis on pattern and color. Plans began on the Harrisonville armory as problems continued to plague the Lone Jack armory in rural Cass County. The Lone Jack armory was a former Nike Missile facility of five separate buildings constructed in 1958. Due to the isolated location, the buildings experienced numerous break-ins. In one robbery, nearly $60,000 worth of equipment was stolen from the facility.

The City of Harrisonville donated the eight-acre site and bids for the armory were opened on July 22, 1986. The design by Gastinger, Rees, and Walker, received the contract for the $1,615,000 armory, which was built by Irvinbilt Construction of Chillicothe, Missouri. The federal government paid $1,252,000 and the State of Missouri $362,000 for the 18,000-square-foot armory and 3,874-square-foot Organizational Maintenance Shop building. The new armory has administrative offices, classrooms, a drill hall, locker and shower areas, a rifle range, a kitchen, and storage space.[13]

Although the Guard wanted a bigger armory at Harrisonville, a federal funding deadline meant the armory was built with the funds available, resulting in a building that is a scaled-down version of the original

12. John Ashcroft to Henry Wallendorf, October 14, 1982, Armory correspondence files, MMMH.

13. Paul L. Junkans, "Information Paper," September 12, 1986, Lexington folder, MNGFE.

design. According to one official, the building is complete and serviceable, but the interior is "austere."[14] The armory was completed in January 1988, and dedicated six months later on June 10, 1988. About five hundred citizens and several dignitaries, including US Congressman Ike Skelton, attended the dedication.[15]

Harrisonville is unusual in two ways from other Missouri armories. The use of building color and window treatment are atypical for an armory. The combination of color and a large glazed surface is attributed to the architect, Wade Walker, who preferred to use vibrant colors and angles in his designs. The Missouri Guard requested his bright color scheme be more muted, which resulted in a pleasant but still colorful building.[16]

Fig. 6.6: Battery C, 128th Field Artillery Armory, 1997

1306 Locust Street, Boonville, Cooper County

Style: traditional revival

Built 1989; occupied 1990–present

Architect: Gould and Evans / Builder: Crawford Construction

Photo: Chuck MacFall

A good example of the traditional revival category, the Boonville armory is a combination of traditional elements and modern materials that communicates the look of a meaningful function inside. This armory is the culmination of many years' effort by city leaders and guardsmen to procure a state-owned armory for Boonville. The funds were allotted in 1988 and construction began on the $950,000 building in March 1989.[17] The 18,000-square-foot facility was completed in 1989, ahead of the scheduled 1990 date. It was built by Crawford Construction on plans by Gould and Evans.

The interior offices and space are arranged in a standard layout. The central drill floor and rooms around it form the traditional U-shape with a large vehicle entrance on the east side. The north arm of the U-shape has a mess hall and supply room, the west side has the entrance and four offices, two on each side of the entry, and the southern arm has an office and arms vault.

14. Paul L. Junkans to Robert Wiegers, June 12, 2007.

15. "Armory Dedication," *Cass County Democrat-Missourian*, June 10, 1988.

16. Paul L. Junkans to Robert Wiegers, personal communication, June 12, 2007.

17. "Boonville National Guard Armory," *Boonville Daily News*, June 9–10, 1989.

Fig. 6.7: Howard M. Garrett Memorial Armory, 1997
2740 West Highway P, Festus, Jefferson County
Style: traditional revival
Built 1989; occupied 1991–present
Architect: Abdelmach Associates / Builder: John B. Harms and Associates
Photo: Chuck MacFall

The Festus armory was built as a replacement for a local WPA armory building. It is a bold example of the traditional revival style with its dominant central entrance and stepped parapet. In June 1985, the City of Festus sold forty acres of land to the State of Missouri for ten dollars. In order to raise the building above the hundred-year flood plain, the 220th Engineers raised the site four feet. This task took nearly 3,000 man-days and 15,000 cubic yards of fill. The armory's design is similar to the postmodern Vanna Venturi House designed in 1961 by Robert Venturi. The new 23,670-square-foot armory project cost $1,309,500, of which the federal government paid $927,000 and the state provided $382,500. It was dedicated on June 8, 1991.[18]

Fig. 6.8: Detachment 1, 1107th AVCAD* Armory, 1997
301 West Fremont, Lebanon, Laclede County
Style: traditional revival
Built 1989; occupied 1989–present
Architect/builder: Sides Construction
Photo: Chuck MacFall
*AVCAD = Aviation Classification Repair Activity Depot

18.   "New Armory Gets Tentative Senate OK," *Jefferson County Journal*, June 14, 1988; and "National Guard Honors Former Rep. Garrett," *Sullivan's Independent News*, June 26, 1991.

Fig. 6.9: Company C, 203rd Engineer Battalion Armory, 1997

300 Chapel Drive, Monett, Barry County

Style: traditional revival

Built 1989; occupied 1992–present

Architect: Russ Williams / Builder: Dalton-Dillinger Construction

Photo: Wiegers

This large armory combines all the elements of the traditional revival style in a linear collection of angles and rooflines. In 1985, the Monett Industrial Development Corporation sold 9.82 acres to the State of Missouri for a new armory. It was another four years before the groundbreaking ceremony took place on August 5, 1989. The cost for the 24,000-square-foot building was estimated at $1.1 million.[19] The dedication was held in April 1992.

Fig 6.10: Headquarters Missouri National Guard/State Emergency Management Agency/Federal Emergency Management Agency/State Highway Patrol, 1997

2300 Militia Drive, Jefferson City, Cole County

Style: traditional revival

Built 1991; occupied 1992–present

Architect: HOK Architects / Builder: BSI Construction

Photo: Chuck MacFall

This armory represents the first time in its history that the Missouri National Guard has had a headquarters facility designed for its use and expansion in the future. In 1988, a section of land consisting of 350 acres was transferred from the Department of Corrections and Human Resources to the Department of Public Safety, Office of the Adjutant General.[20] The land had been part of a 770-acre farm operated by

19. "Groundbreaking Saturday for New $1.1 Million Armory," *Monett* (MO) *Times*, August 1, 1989.

20. Memorandum of Agreement between the Department of Corrections and Human Resources and the Department of Public Safety-National Guard, April 27, 1988, Jefferson City Headquarters/Algoa folder, MNGFE.

the Missouri Penal System since the 1930s.[21] The transfer allowed the Missouri Guard to build a facility for property storage, the Office of the Adjutant General of Missouri, the State Area Command Headquarters, and other facilities.[22]

Once the property was acquired, construction of the new structures began in phases. The first phase entailed the construction of office and warehouse space for the United States Property and Fiscal Office, and a Combined Support Maintenance Shop and Organizational Maintenance Shop, all of which were partially or fully funded by the federal government. The Adjutant General's Office was 100 percent state funded.[23]

Today the Missouri Guard Headquarters sits atop a bluff overlooking the Missouri River several miles south of Jefferson City. The complex consists of a three-story, all brick headquarters building built around a central courtyard. Surrounding it are offices, a mess hall, medical facilities, classrooms, and storage. The State Emergency Management Office and Federal Emergency Management Office occupy a portion of the facility and the State Highway Patrol maintains a practice-driving track. A section of the complex is devoted to a traditional Guard unit with its own offices, storage, armory, and drill hall. Arranged around the main complex are maintenance shops, warehouses, motor pools, and a Missouri National Guard museum.

Fig. 6.11: Rolf Raynor Armory, 1997

5151 North Roger Wilson, Columbia, Boone County

Style: traditional revival

Built 1995; occupied 1996–present

Architect: Jack D. Ball and Associates / Builder: Professional Contractors and Engineers, Inc.

Photo: Chuck MacFall

21. Memorandum of Agreement between the Department of Corrections and Human Resources and the Department of Public Safety-National Guard, April 27, 1988, Jefferson City Headquarters/Algoa folder, MNGFE.

22. Order of Reassignment of Space, from the Department of Corrections and Human Resources to the Department of Public Safety-National Guard, April 27, 1988, Jefferson City Headquarters/Algoa folder, MNGFE.

23. Charles M. Kiefner to the Honorable Marvin Proffer, "Facilities," February 24, 1988, Jefferson City Headquarters/Algoa folder, MNGFE.

Fig. 6.12: Captain John W. "Jack" Haggarty Memorial Armory, 1997
First Attack Drive, Whiteman Air Force Base, Knob Noster, Johnson County
Style: traditional revival
Built 1995; occupied 1997–present
Architect: Guenther-Mills / Builder: M. A. Mortenson Construction
Photo: Wiegers

Fig. 6.13: Brigadier General O. T. Dalton Jr. and Captain William Anderson Jr.
Memorial Armory, 1998
986 Iowa Drive, Fort Leonard Wood, Pulaski County
Style: traditional revival
Built 1996; occupied 1997–present
Architect: Gastinger, Walker, and Hardin / Builder: Kloster Building Group
Photo: Chuck MacFall

Fig. 6.14: F. A. Findley Memorial Armory, 2004
1605 Cravens Road, Poplar Bluff, Butler County
Style: traditional revival
Built 1997; occupied 1997–present
Architect: Robert Sterns / Builder: Huffman Construction
Photo: Wiegers

Fig. 6.15: Colonel Blees Armory, 2003
1616 South Missouri Street, Macon, Macon County
Style: traditional revival
Built 2001; occupied 2001–present
Architect: Veldhuizen and Livingston / Builder: LICO Construction
Photo: Wiegers

This armory incorporates many aspects of the modern style into a traditional building. It is a one-story building with few windows and a standing-seam metal roof. The formal entrance is offset to the left of center, which balances out the half-story drill-hall roof area. It was built in 2001 by LICO Construction of Kansas City, with architect Ivan Livingston of Kansas City. The armory was dedicated on August 19, 2001.

Fig. 6.16: 129th Field Artillery Armory and Maryville Community Center, 2003
1407 North Country Club Road, Maryville, Nodaway County
Style: traditional revival
Built 2002; occupied 2003–present
Architect/builder: Shaughnessy, Fickel and Scott Assoc.
Photo: MMMH

Fig. 6.17: McLaughlin Memorial Armory, 2005
2001 Clarendon Road, Sedalia, Pettis County
Style: traditional revival
Built 2003; occupied 2003–present
Architect/builder: Shaughnessy, Fickel and Scott Assoc.
Photo: Wiegers

Fig. 6.18: 1221st Transportation Company Armory, 2010
1702 State Highway 114, Dexter, Stoddard County
Style: traditional revival
Built 2006; occupied 2006–present
Architect/builder: Robert Starnes and Associates
Photo: Missouri National Guard

Fig. 6.19: PFC Lawrence A. Witt Memorial Armory, 2010
600 South Pine Street, Pierce City, Lawrence County
Style: traditional revival
Built 2006; occupied 2006–present
Architect/builder: Gossen Livingston Associates
Photo: Wiegers

Fig. 6.20: Joint Armed Forces Reserve Center, 2010
24 Davis Street, St. Louis Jefferson Barracks, St. Louis County
Style: traditional revival
Built 2010; occupied 2010–present
Architect: Ross and Baruzzini / Builder: K & S Associates
Photo: Bill Phelan

The latest addition to the inventory of Missouri National Guard armories is officially named the Joint Armed Forces Reserve Center since it incorporates the dual usage concept between the Guard and the Army Reserve. The building was designed by architects Ross and Baruzzini to blend into the built environment of historic Jefferson Barracks. The multistory, red brick building holds 280,500 square feet of training, administration, and maintenance space.[24]

24. Bill Phelan, "Missouri National Guard to Unveil Joint Armed Forces Reserve Center," *Bear Facts*, Fall 2010, 14.

Chapter 7
Architectural Gems
The Unique Category

Over the years, a number of buildings in Missouri were built or used as National Guard armories that did not evolve in unison with Guard requirements. These one-of-a-kind styles and vernacular armories are examples of unique architecture that warrant inclusion in this volume. A commonality among these buildings is the happenstance nature of how they were brought into the Guard inventory. Whenever a new unit was organized or Missouri Guard units shuffled about, a new home was needed and these buildings were available. They may have been built for a different purpose, therefore some are odd fits for the Guard, but some are ideally suited to the needs of the Guard and a few are genuinely versatile designs that incorporate both functionality and beauty in one building.

Some of the buildings in this category have thrust the Missouri National Guard into a position of steward to Missouri heritage buildings. The Guard may not have intended to be a keeper of historic buildings, but in some cases, that role is a serendipitous byproduct of Guard presence in communities scattered around the state. Often the most available building for a new Guard unit is an older and larger but still serviceable building that might have been demolished due to neglect were it not for the Guard.

Currently the Missouri Guard serves as a keeper of Missouri heritage in the French eclectic style orphanage in Carrollton and in the old warehouse and associated structures at Camp Clark. Even if the Guard does not hold these unique properties indefinitely, Guard ownership will extend their life and perhaps help them into a new usage in the built environment. Temporary stewardship of historic properties is not a dilemma for the Guard as long as the building is serviceable and contributes visually to the Guard image. Also included in the unique category are a number of the Missouri Air National Guard buildings and hangars, also called the Air Service at one time. Although the Air Service armories are vernacular buildings, aircraft hangars are unlike anything in the Guard building tradition and their story is slightly divergent from the mainstream of armory construction, making it appropriate to include them in the unique category.

Inventory of Unique Armories and Architectural Gems (by date built)

Fig. 7.1: Bequet-Ribault House, 1985
Similar to Missouri Militia Meeting House/Yosti House, 1808
Main and Locust Streets, St. Louis
Style: French Colonial
Built: 1766; occupied 1808 as militia meeting house
Architect/builder: Alexis Marie
Photo: Historic American Building Survey

Topping the list of unique armories in Missouri is the oldest documented militia armory in Missouri—the St. Louis home and business of Italian immigrant and Santa Fe trader Emelien Yosti. According to National Park Service records, the house was built in 1766 in the French colonial style by Frenchman Alexis Marie, who lived in the house until 1781, when he sold it to Yosti.[1] The building, which held both Yosti's home and his business, was a thirty-by-twenty-two-foot *poteaux en terre* vertical log house. The building was substantial enough to host the Court of Quarter Sessions in 1804 and to act as headquarters for the local militia as early as 1808.[2]

Most likely the house was a single-story dwelling, similar in size and shape to the Bequet-Ribault House in Ste. Genevieve, Missouri. The Yosti family probably lived in half of the house and used the other half for commercial storage and for their tavern business. A large attic and possible cellars for storage complemented the business aspect of the structure. The Yosti House was razed sometime prior to 1860.

The Bequet-Ribault House (shown here) was built in the traditional French colonial style using building techniques similar to those common twenty-three years earlier when the Alexis Marie/Yosti house was built. The Bequet-Ribault House has not been greatly altered, and was renovated in 1985 when the galleries on four sides were restored.

1. Schart, *History of St. Louis City and County*, 1:146.
2. Hyde and Conard, *Encyclopedia of the History of St. Louis*, 1:2566.

Fig. 7.2: Battery A/Verandah Row Armory, stereoscope, ca. 1880

Washington and Fourth Street, St. Louis

Style: steamboat Gothic

Built: 1853; occupied by militia ca. 1878

Architect/builder: William McPherson and Barton Bates

Photo: Robert N. Dennis Collection of Stereoscopic Views, Miriam and Ira D. Wallach Division of Art, Prints and Photographs, The New York Public Library, Astor, Lenox and Tilden Foundations

In the tradition of rental armories, the famous St. Louis Light Battery A rented this fancy building in its waning days of use. The series of storefronts was called Verandah Row because of the overhead full-length balcony that sheltered pedestrians from rain or sun. The general style is called steamboat Gothic, an allusion to the style's inspiration in the decorative details of ornate balconies and wheelhouses of river steamboats, which were copied for buildings along the Mississippi River. Buildings in this style are typically two stories tall, with elaborate and ornate scrollwork decorations on porches and galleries.

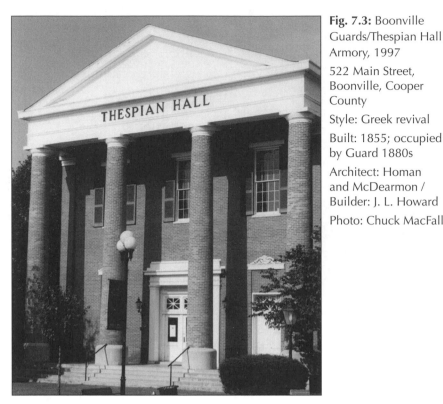

Fig. 7.3: Boonville Guards/Thespian Hall Armory, 1997

522 Main Street, Boonville, Cooper County

Style: Greek revival

Built: 1855; occupied by Guard 1880s

Architect: Homan and McDearmon / Builder: J. L. Howard

Photo: Chuck MacFall

    Thespian Hall was constructed between 1855 and 1857 as a community reading room and theater building. It is two stories tall with a formal entrance flanked by four prominent Doric brick columns supporting a monumental portico. The basement level is believed to have been used by the Boonville Guards as an armory in the late nineteenth century. The Boonville Guards and another local unit, the Waddill Guard, used Thespian Hall for competitive drills around the turn of the century.[3] Thespian Hall is on the National Register of Historic Places.

3. "Waddill Guards," *Boonville Weekly Advertiser*, February 27, 1880.

Fig. 7.4: Lindell Grays, Taylor Guards/Four Courts Armory, ca. 1875

Clark Avenue, Spruce, Eleventh, and Twelfth Streets, St. Louis

Style: Second Empire

Built: 1871; occupied by militia ca. 1870s–1880s

Architect/builder: Thomas P. Walsh

Photo: Robert N. Dennis Collection of Stereoscopic Views, Miriam and Ira D. Wallach Division of Art, Prints and Photographs, The New York Public Library, Astor, Lenox and Tilden Foundations

The misnamed Four Courts Building stood on the spot of the former Henri Chouteau Mansion, which overlooked the newly industrialized Chouteau's Mill Creek area in St. Louis. The building did hold the St. Louis Criminal Court, the Court of Criminal Corrections, and the Police Court, as well as the city marshal and other officials, but the name was derived from the similarity between the St. Louis building and the infamous "four courts" of Dublin, Ireland. Various units of the Missouri Militia used the building as an armory during riots in the city. The building was razed in 1907 due to structural problems.

Fig. 7.5: Company G, Fourth Infantry Armory/former Methodist Episcopal Church
South, 1910

1107 East Broadway, Columbia, Boone County

Style: ecclesiastical Gothic revival

Built 1872; occupied by Guard 1910–1913

Architect/builder unknown

Photo: *Biennial Report of the Adjutant General 1909–1910*

The former Methodist Episcopal Church South in Columbia was a National Guard armory in the early 1900s. In 1871 the Methodist Episcopal Church South built a new church to replace a smaller one. The new church, built in the ecclesiastical Gothic style, opened for services in 1872 and was formally dedicated in 1875. The total cost of construction was $20,000, and at the time of its completion, the church had the tallest spire in the City of Columbia.[4]

By 1900, the congregation had outgrown this building and it was sold to local businessman J. K. Fyfer. It had several different uses, including housing an entertainment hall and a printing press, before the Guard took over on March 5, 1910.[5] The Guard stayed in the former church building until 1913, but the building was known locally as "armory hall" for many years afterward. The building was razed sometime between 1915 and 1921.

---

4. Stephens, *History of the Missouri Methodist Church of Columbia*, 80–81.

5. Adjutant General, *Biennial Report ... 1909–1910*, 414.

Fig. 7.6: First Infantry Regiment Armory/Armory Hall, ca. 1890
Pine and 18th Streets, St. Louis
Style: Second Empire
Built 1881; occupied 1882–ca. 1900
Architect: Miller and Pitcher / Builder: Barnes and Morrison
Photo: MHS-STL

The St. Louis Armory Hall was possibly the largest privately built armory in the city. The building at Pine and 18th Streets was designed by Miller and Pitcher and built by Barnes and Morrison. Over the years it was used by the Guard, it was home to a number of militia companies in the city, including Companies A, E, F, and G of the First Infantry. This large urban armory was originally built to house a newly established National Guard presence in the city. The cornerstone was laid in 1881 and the building was finished enough to be used for drills by 1882. The rent for the armory ground was $1,200 per year and the total cost of the armory construction was expected to be more than $70,000, paid for by popular subscription in the City of St. Louis. With a footprint of 195 by 109 feet, the building was three stories at the front and two stories at either end and rear. It contained one cavalry and one infantry drill room on the ground floor, and twenty-one large company and regimental rooms, stables, and an artillery park on the two lower floors. The top floor is a large drill hall of 109 by 104 feet, capable of holding 4,500 chairs. The weight of the top floor was carried on sixteen heavy cross trusses and a central longitudinal truss system. The roof is one span of 107 feet that rises to sixty feet and is capped by a tin roof. Four hundred gas jets connected to lamps and chandeliers provided illumination for the large drill hall.[6] The building was razed circa 1945.

6. Adjutant General, *Report … to the 32nd General Assembly*, 18–23.

Fig. 7.7: Former Company C, 175th Military Police Battalion Armory, 1997
Stone Cottage, East Morgan Street, Boonville, Cooper County
Style: Queen Anne
Built 1894; occupied by Guard 1983–1989
Architect/builder unknown
Photo: Chuck MacFall

Stone Cottage was built on the grounds of the Missouri Training School for Boys as a dormitory and classroom building in 1894. Similar to its twin (Stephens Cottage) a mere twenty yards away, Stone Cottage was a two-story brick building in the Queen Anne style. Shortly after the Boonville Guard moved into the Stone Cottage, a movement was underway in Congress (HB 601) to allocate federal and state money to build new armories.[7] In 1988, construction began on a new armory and in 1989, the Boonville Guard unit moved into its first state-owned home.

Fig. 7.8: Former Battery A, 128th Field Artillery Armory Building 26, 1997
Sherman Road, St. Louis Jefferson Barracks, St. Louis County
Style: federal
Built 1896; occupied by Guard 1973–1994
Architect/builder: US Army Quartermaster Corps, Standardized Plan #41
Photo: Chuck MacFall

7. Dave Para, "House Bill Would Give Guard a New, Permanent Armory," *Boonville Daily News*, March 10, 1983.

St. Louis's famous Light Artillery Battery, renamed Battery A, 128th Field Artillery, searched for a permanent home after it left the armory built for it by the St. Louis Light Artillery Armory Association on South Grand Avenue. The unit quartered for a short time at the Market Street armory of the 138th Infantry and then, in 1973, found quarters in Double Barracks 26 bordering the famous parade ground at Jefferson Barracks in St. Louis County. What should have been a permanent home became a twenty-year stay in 1994 when the unit was decommissioned.

The barracks armory of Battery A was part of the 1893 to 1902 construction effort at Jefferson Barracks to replace antiquated pre–Civil War quarters with modern infantry accommodations. A series of red brick double barracks were constructed along the south side of the parade ground according to US Army Quartermaster Corps designs, Standardized Plan #41. Today, Jefferson Barracks is much reduced in size and is maintained by the Missouri Air National Guard.

Fig. 7.9: Stephens Cottage, Boonville Correctional Center/ former Company C, 175th Military Police Battalion Armory, 1997

East Morgan Street, Boonville, Cooper County

Style: Queen Anne

Built 1896; occupied by Guard 1981–1983

Architect/builder unknown

Photo: Chuck MacFall

In the continuing saga of Missouri National Guard units moving in search of a home, one Boonville unit moved to a convenient but unusual location. In 1981, the Boonville Guard moved to a new drill location in Stephens Cottage located on the grounds of the Missouri Training School for Boys, a correctional institution for youthful offenders. The move was prompted by declining enlistments in the post-Vietnam era, and the move to Stephens Cottage saved the unit over $7,000 annually in rent.[8] The building was built in 1896 to house a dormitory and classrooms. Now it provided the Guard unit with more space than it had in its previous location. All fourteen of the Guard's vehicles were housed in a nearby building. In 1983, the Guard unit was once again forced to move when the Training School was turned over to the Department of Corrections and was slated to become a prison; Stephens Cottage was to become part of the new entrance to the facility.

8. Doug Whitaker, "Local National Guard Unit Plans Move to Training School," *Boonville Daily News*, July 3–4, 1981.

Fig. 7.10: 735th Ordnance Battalion Armory, 1953
West High Street, Jefferson City, Cole County
Style: Greek revival
Built ca. 1900; occupied by Guard 1953–ca. 1960
Architect/builder unknown
Photo: MMMH

This classical structure was built around 1900 for the Missouri Public Service Commission, and was located close to the Missouri State Capitol building. When the Public Service Commission moved into the new Jefferson Building in 1953, the Guard acquired the facility.[9] The Greek revival, two-story stone building was unusual for Guard use, and served as an armory for only a short time. It is the most high-style classical revival armory the Guard has occupied in Missouri. The building was razed in the late 1960s.

9. "National Guard Acquires New Armory."

Fig. 7.11: American Legion Post 69/former Battery F, 203rd Coast Artillery Armory, 2000

149 Memorial Place, Springfield, Greene County

Style: Italian revival

Built ca. 1900; occupied by Guard 1939–1941

Architect/builder: Louis Repp

Photo: Wiegers

The oldest part of American Legion Post 69 is a two-story house donated to the Legion by local businessman Louis Repp. The Charles Holland house is a substantial residence moved to the present location in the 1920s. The current complex consists of the original Holland House with a basement and second-floor auditorium, and a museum on the top floor. It was not unusual for the Missouri Guard to lease space in American Legion or VFW halls when a state-owned facility was not available.

Fig. 7.12: Dockery Building/former Headquarters Company, Thirty-fifth Division Armory, 1997

Central Missouri State University, Warrensburg, Johnson County

Style: Romanesque

Built 1904; occupied by Guard 1939–1941

Architect: George E. McDonald / Builder: Moore Brothers and MacDonald

Photo: Chuck MacFall

Originally constructed as a college gym, today the Dockery Building is the oldest building on the campus of Central Missouri State University and houses a number of academic programs, from computers to accountancy. The Missouri Guard leased space in the old gym to train recruits and house its equipment prior to the outbreak of World War II.

Fig. 7.13: Camp Clark Armory, State Rifle Range, 1997
Bldg. 131/132, Camp Clark, Nevada, Vernon County
Style: vernacular
Built 1909; occupied 1909–present
Architect/builder: Black and Veach
Photo: Wiegers

The Camp Clark National Guard warehouse and armory is the oldest structure still standing built by the Missouri National Guard. The warehouse was built in 1909 on a portion of the 640 acres purchased by the state in 1908. The warehouse was part of a complex that included a training ground and a 1,000-yard shooting range. The warehouse was originally brick on a stone foundation, fifty feet wide and one hundred feet long, adjacent to a rail siding running to Nevada, Missouri. The warehouse was probably built under the supervision of Major C. G. Synms in 1908/09 at a cost of $3,600.[10] In the late 1970s, part of the warehouse was converted into an armory, but today the warehouse is used primarily for storage. Since the warehouse has served a number of purposes—storage, offices, and armory—the interior and exterior have been greatly altered. The original flat-roofed rectangular structure is now covered with a stucco finish.

Fig. 7.14: Battery A, 128th Field Artillery Armory/Mess Hall, Building 78, 1998
Davis Street, Mess Hall, St. Louis Jefferson Barracks, St. Louis County
Style: Standard Plan #41
Built 1912; occupied by Guard 1994–2010
Architect/builder: US Army Quartermaster Corps, Standardized Plan #2-1003
Photo: Chuck MacFall

The Jefferson Barracks Mess Hall was built in 1912 from plans designed by the US Army Quarter-master Corps after the old mess hall, Building 36, proved inadequate for the 1,000 trainees and 300

10. "Camp Clark History," on file at Camp Clark, Missouri National Guard, Nevada, Missouri.

permanent personnel.[11] The new structure, Building 78, was to be two stories with a partial basement and a clear, open dining area designed to serve two purposes. Its primary purpose was a post mess hall with food storage, lavatories, and dish-washing space in the basement area and a dining hall on the main floor. Designed to accommodate 1,200 personnel, this building was at one time the largest space on post and it therefore served a second purpose—it was used as an instructional and classroom area and a general post assembly point.

The second floor over the 52-by-84-foot kitchen area was a dorm for the cooks. Two service elevators connected the main dining area with the cleanup area and storage below. Since it was anticipated that during dining hours there would be a rush into and out of the building, the building had entryways on three sides. Stupp Brothers Bridge and Iron Company supplied the steel support elements in the building. The heating system was installed by Urbauer-Atwood Heating Company for $7,360, and the cooking apparatus came from Wrought Iron Range Company for $5,694.15. The whole structure cost $90,432.15.[12] The building was used as an armory from 1994 to 2010.

Fig. 7.15: Former Presser Hall Armory, 1997
Hardin College, Mexico, Audrain County
Style: neoclassical
Built 1926; occupied by Guard 1930s and possibly 1940s
Architect: Bonsack and Pearce / Builder: McCarthy Brothers Construction
Photo: Chuck MacFall

In the 1930s, Hardin College, a former private college in Mexico, Missouri, that closed in 1931, rented space to the Missouri National Guard in the Presser Hall Conservatory of Music for an armory. The building had been a gift to the college from the Presser Foundation of Philadelphia and cost $115,000 to build. The interior held nine studios, twenty-five practice rooms, and a large music room. The auditorium was large enough to seat fourteen hundred on the main floor with additional seating in two balconies. The auditorium was also equipped to serve as a movie theatre.[13] The building was used as an armory during the 1930s and possibly the early part of the 1940s. The buildings and grounds of the former Hardin College are now owned by the City of Mexico.

11. Captain/Quartermaster to Quartermaster General, January 3, 1910, and Quartermaster General to Adjutant General, February 7, 1910, both from Quartermaster General 1800–1914 Document File, RG92, National Archives.

12. Esley Hamilton, St. Louis County Department of Parks and Recreation, to Suzanne Murphy, October 13, 1997, attachment: "Notes on New Mess Hall" (copy in author's files).

13. Hardin College, *The Ion, 1926*, Mexico Public Library, Mexico, Missouri.

Fig. 7.16: Company C, 135th Signal Battalion Armory, 1997
Route 1, Carrollton, Carroll County
Style: French eclectic
Built 1936; occupied by Guard 1989–present
Architect/builder: Charles A. Haskins
Photo: Chuck MacFall

A leased building, the Carrollton armory is one of the most appealing examples of armory architecture in the state. The former orphanage, a striking example of French eclectic architecture, is situated in a county park with ample room for outdoor training. In 1921, the Missouri State Board of Charities purchased the forty-acre site from Mrs. Laura Turpin for the establishment of a state school for ill-treated and homeless children to be operated by the Eleemosynary Department.[14] The New Boys Cottage was built by architect Charles A. Haskins and dedicated on October 25, 1936.[15] The 25,000-square-foot building was built with funds from the Federal Emergency Administration, a predecessor to the WPA. Later the orphanage was merged with the state school at Marshall and the cottage was turned into the State School No. 2 for boys and girls who were mentally handicapped. In 1975, the state sold the buildings and land to the City of Carrollton for public use. The cottage was used for various purposes, then stood vacant for ten years until January 1, 1989, when the Missouri National Guard assumed control through a thirty-year lease for one dollar per year. The new armory became the home of Detachment 2, Company B, 135th Signal Battalion, later Company C, 135th Signal Battalion.[16] Seventy-five years after Mrs. Turpin sold the original land to the state, the area known as Walnut Hill is still serving the community and the Missouri National Guard.

14. Warranty Deed, November 4, 1921, Carroll County, MO, Book 250, Page 207, Carrollton folder, MNGFE.

15. "New Boy's Cottage Dedicated," *Carrollton Daily Democrat*, October 26, 1936.

16. "Carrollton's National Guard Unit Getting Organized," *Carrollton Daily Democrat*, February 15, 1989.

Fig. 7.17: Headquarters Company, 140th Infantry, 1998
Old Route 67/South Highway OO, Farmington, St. Francois County
Style: Quonset hut
Built ca. 1941; occupied by Guard ca. 1949
Architect/builder: George A. Fuller Company
Photo: Chuck MacFall

As America prepared for World War II, there was a need for prefabricated housing that was equal to or better than the British Nissen hut. A design team from the George A. Fuller Company designed and built the first huts at Quonset Point Naval Air Station, Rhode Island; hence the name. The Quonset was a curved design formed by steel ribs and covered with corrugated metal with plywood flooring. Insulation was provided by a Masonite filler between ribs and paper wadding. The hut came in two basic sizes: for a twenty-man unit and a forty-man unit. The smaller size was twenty feet wide and forty-eight feet long. Often Quonset huts were arranged or adapted for use by joining two either side by side or end to end.[17]

This structure was built in about 1941 for use during the war years. After the war, the building was owned by the East Central Missouri Hereford Breeders Association, which sold it to the Guard in about 1949. This armory is actually two huts joined to make one building with a total of three thousand square feet of floor space. Around 1949, National Guard Headquarters Company, Second Battalion, 140th Infantry, moved into its temporary home in this temporary building.[18] Today, the structure is used by retail business.

17. See Chiei and Decker, *Quonset Hut.*
18. "Local Nat'l Guard to Soon Have New Home," *Farmington News,* October 21, 1949.

Fig. 7.18: Thirty-fifth Engineer Brigade Armory/Fort Leonard Wood, 1997
1200 area, Iowa Avenue, Fort Leonard Wood, Pulaski County
Style: 700 and 800 Series Cantonment Construction
Built ca. 1941; occupied by Guard 1993–1998
Architect/builder: US Army Quartermaster Corps
Photo: Chuck MacFall

In 1993, efforts materialized to move the headquarters and Headquarters Company, Thirty-fifth Engineer Brigade from historic Jefferson Barracks in St. Louis to new facilities in Fort Leonard Wood. The move was necessary because it would allot the Missouri Guard engineer unit access to the new US Army Engineer Center and School located at Fort Leonard Wood.

In March 1993, eleven World War II barracks and support buildings constructed between 1941 and 1943 were inspected for Guard use. Seven of these were one-story (700 series) and four were two-story (800 series) wood buildings. Although dated, the buildings were "rehabilitated with insulated metal siding, thermal pane windows, new roofs, and other energy efficient modifications."[19] In the later part of 1993, the Thirty-fifth Engineer Brigade began its move to a temporary home in the 1200 area not very far from the future site of their new armory on Iowa Avenue.

19. Raymond L. Pendergrass, Memorandum to Major General W. Christman, Commanding General, US Army Engineer Center and Fort Leonard Wood, 25 March 1993, Leonard Wood folder, MNGFE.

Fig. 7.19: 1139th Military Police Company/Nike Missile Site 30, ca. 1970
State Road KK, Lone Jack, Cass County
Style: complex of buildings in military vernacular
Built 1958; occupied by Guard 1969–1988
Architect/builder: US Army Corps of Engineers
Photo: Walt Wilson

The Lone Jack armory was a fine example of adaptive reuse of a former federal facility for a National Guard armory. Unfortunately, armories created from old installations and sites far from a local community often had little connection to the community and little to identify them as National Guard buildings. The Lone Jack armory was part of the former Nike Missile Site control and administrative center. This cantonment was built during the early Cold War era as part of a larger complex that included detached sites for missile-firing batteries. This particular site contained four one-story rectangular block buildings, each serving a specific function, such as a barracks building, mess hall, or operations center, with separate radar stands and maintenance buildings.

The Guard acquired this site in 1969 as a training area and temporary armory until a new armory could be built. Several of the former barracks and administrative buildings were converted to National Guard use. The isolated rural setting of the site did not make it the best location for an armory because of security issues. In 1986, the local newspaper reported that the facility had been burglarized three times in the past year, losing about $60,000 in equipment, but no weapons of any type.[20] In 1987, the new Harrisonville armory was completed and the Lone Jack site was decommissioned. The building is currently privately owned.

20. "Thefts from Armory Total $60,000 Loss," *Cass County Democrat-Missourian*, June 10, 1986.

Army Air Service National Guard Armories

In 1947 the US Air Force became a separate uniform service apart from the US Army Air Corps. At the same time, the National Guard also fielded an air service. Based in larger cities, the Guard Air Service occupied several buildings as armories and built several hangars that are uncommon in the Missouri Guard inventory of facilities.

Expanded use of the airplane in military strategy led to the establishment of the US Army Air Corps on June 4, 1920. This necessitated accommodating the new technology in the National Guard by locating Guard units adjacent to airfields and constructing hangars. But the Guard Air Service required more than just an armory; it needed a large covered space for storage and maintenance, as well as an airstrip. St. Louis was the first Guard Air Service base in Missouri because of local public

interest in aviation and because of the newly purchased St. Louis-Lambert Field. In 1931, the city voted a bond issue of $75,000 to construct a hangar and an administration building for the Thirty-fifth Division Air Service.[21]

When the Thirty-fifth Division Air Service formally organized on June 23, 1923, St. Louis became home to the Air Guard. Air corps Guard units assigned to St. Louis were the 110th Observation Squadron, the 110th Photo Section, the 110th Medical Detachment, and the 170th Intelligence Section (which was later amalgamated with the Photo Section). Prior to settling at the Lambert Field facility, the 110th moved six times to different buildings. The first recorded building they used was a 1923 gasoline station on Manchester Road in present day St. Louis County. The second was a small room over a "grocery store on Olive Road in St. Louis County" in the same year (see fig. 7.20). The third building they used was a large room at 115 Hodiamont Avenue on the second floor of a store building. The fourth was at 200 Theresa Avenue in "an old and unsightly factory building."[22] Apparently this last was so bad that the 110th moved into temporary quarters with Light Battery A on South Grand Avenue in 1927 to await a new armory and maintain its active unit status.[23] A sixth armory

Fig. 7.20: Thirty-fifth Division Aviation Armory, ca. 1920

Olive Street, St. Louis

Style: vernacular

Built ca. 1900; occupied by Guard 1920–1925

Architect/builder unknown

Photo: MMMH

---

21. City of St. Louis Ordinance 38329, March 14, 1930, attachment to Ray H. Green to Arthur R. Wilson, Headquarters Jefferson Barracks, Office of the Quartermaster, December 28, 1939, Air Guard armory file, MMMH.

22. Armory Inspection Report, March 22, 1927, Armory correspondence files, MMMH.

23. C. R. Wassall to Paul C. Hunt, May 3, 1927, Armory correspondence files, MMMH.

was found for the 110th at 208 South Twelfth Street in 1929. This building served until their final move in 1931 to Lambert Field (see fig. 7.21).[24] The Air Guard maintains the hangar and other facilities there today.

As a part of the Thirty-fifth Division of the Missouri National Guard, the 110th was comprised of three elements totaling twenty-two officers and one hundred enlisted men; their most famous member was Lieutenant Charles Lindbergh. In 1934, the 110th armory consisted of a hangar large enough for eight military planes, office space for operations, a machine shop, supply room, flight surgeon, dispensary, and a boiler room. Also included were a tower room on the hangar for administrative space and an officers' club. A hangar mezzanine housed the aerial lab, a classroom for one hundred men, the communication and repair section, an armament room, and a supply room. A separate building contained lockers for enlisted men and a club. Another building, a quarter the size of the hangar, was under construction and would be used for vehicles and office space.

In 1935, the National Guard Association was heavily involved in promoting inclusion of an armory-building program in WPA appropriations. As part of this effort, the St. Louis Observation Squadron submitted a request for funding for a project that included a hangar, an administration building, a gasoline distribution system for a 25,000-gallon tank, and 3,300 feet of pipeline with associated pumps and pits.

For communities striving to improve their aviation image, securing a National Guard aviation unit was a great advantage; it was also a convenient way to upgrade local airport facilities. When knowledge surfaced of a new Guard aviation unit in the state, Kansas City and St. Joseph were spurred to action to outbid each other to host the unit. Rosecrans Field at St. Joseph offered four concrete runways, taxiways, nightlights, and a Class A rating from the Civil Aeronautical Authority. The city was willing to lease space to the Guard for ninety-nine years if requested.[25] Kansas City was not to be outdone. Its airport boasted four runways, the longest being 5,400 feet long by 150 feet wide. It was also willing to lease land on the field.[26] St. Joseph was eventually chosen to host the unit.

Fig. 7.21: Thirty-fifth Division Aviation Hangar, 1939
St. Louis-Lambert International Airport, St. Louis
Style: hangar
Built 1939; occupied 1939–present
Architect/builder unknown
Photo: MMMH

24. Missouri Air Guard, 35th Division, *The Show Me Spirit: A 50 Year History of the Missouri Air National Guard, 1923–1973* (copy in MMMH library).

25. Bradley to Williams, June 18, 1940, Armory correspondence files, MMMH.

26. Catts to Lewis Means, June 1, 1940, Armory correspondence files, MMMH.

Chapter 8
The Missouri National Guard Armory in History and Culture

An unseen but productive dynamic exists between society and the built environment. The interplay begins during construction when we start adapting a space into a building and continues after completion as we adapt the building we have created. The interaction between buildings and society is amplified with the number and size of buildings as we build more and larger buildings. If one building can impact a person's daily routine, then collections of buildings comprising factories and office blocks create activity areas we navigate freely. Sir Winston Churchill understood the bond between mankind and architecture when he noted, "We shape our dwellings and afterwards our dwellings shape us."[1] As we adapt our lives to a new building, we also learn to accept its features as a permanent part of our accustomed surroundings. The new piece of architecture, regardless of its traditional or avant-garde style is accepted as part of our lives—if it survives. The great arbiter of good or bad architecture, regardless of architectural commentary, appears to be time; what endures inherits the aura of antiquity.[2]

As culture-bearing beings, we never fully forget the past. The strength of our collective architectural memory is amazingly strong. Testimonials to the tenacity of that memory surround us in designs and features we unconsciously accept because they are common and embedded in our group history. This is pointedly illustrated by a cartoon published in the Missouri National Guard's periodical the *Bear Facts* in which two guardsmen are speculating about an aircraft, and in the background is a building on a hill representing the Missouri National Guard headquarters. Whereas a box outline with a peaked roof would have indicated a building, the cartoonist wanted to portray in a few strokes the military purpose of the building on the hill. The solution, drawing on traditional designs and functions from cultural memory, was to change the generic box outline into an unmistakable military silhouette by adding a line of crenellations to the flat roof.

Sometime in the future of military construction, new architectural elements from the postmodern or midcentury modern past may displace or rise to the same level of acceptance as current traditional features in Guard armory designs. Perhaps the flat roof and somber brick treatment will come to symbolize a new vision of the National Guard. But until that happens, the traditional forms reign supreme.

---

1. House, *Winston Churchill: His Wit and Wisdom*, 137.
2. Huxtable, *On Architecture*, 243.

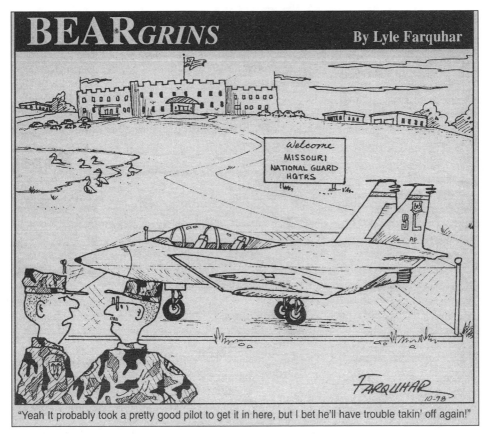

Fig. 8.1: Lyle Farquhar cartoon, *Bear Facts* 23, no. 9 (Feb. 1999): 2.

What lies in the future for armory design? A relapse to Type 783 designs does not appear to be in the offing. Although the U-shaped floor plan of the WPA and Type 783 styles is now a proven footprint, exterior treatment of armory buildings has returned to variety in shapes and colors. Whatever is to come next, we may hope that the style will not return to the austerity of the Cold War.

Community and local Guard involvement in the planning process is the best way to ensure that future armories are equal to the Guard's corporate image. While tracing the recent history of the armory, it is difficult to detect how much bearing local sensitivities have had on armory construction. From 1920 on, it appears once a city expressed interest in acquiring an armory, the community input stopped. On rare occasions, such as the City of Carthage requesting a local stone instead of the standardized Type 783 brick, did the citizenry change the government template for armory design. Perhaps no one asked the community for suggestions or perhaps suggestions the community put forth had little effect.

Public meetings can focus planning attention on a community's views on acceptable styles and suitable building locations. Just as importantly, local voices can reveal preferences in the symbolism, suitable colors, and, very importantly, the naming of a future armory.

The local Guard unit has practical experience with what does and does not work in a Guard armory. While the floor plan may need to fit specific requirements, aesthetic aspects of the design may be influenced by the local Guard unit. Would unit personnel like the new armory to look governmental or more local? What should the interior include to create a comfortable workplace, and what amenities should be built to ensure the future growth of the unit? Local considerations should influence the planning for the best location for the future armory: perhaps the community would most appreciate siting the armory in the inner city with its dual benefits of central location and historical setting, as well as its role as a spark to economic revitalization. In the late twentieth century, the Guard followed the general migration away from the city core; perhaps now is the time to return.

Currently the majority of vernacular armories and all but a few of the WPA armories have been transferred to private hands. Nonetheless, they continue to represent National Guard history. The City of Aurora converted a former armory into office space for the superintendent of schools. The City of Cape Girardeau accepted a spacious armory and converted it into a convention center. The City of Columbia's centrally located art deco armory is now a city recreation center. These successful makeovers to civilian status retain the exterior look and image of the former armory, enduring testimonials to the longevity of the Guard in the community.

The changing demands put on the Guard often require a new armory for a large company. In these circumstances, the old armory is declared inadequate, and a replacement is sought, which may mean leaving a community. This is a weighty decision for the Guard with great impact on the community, since a decision to leave an established armory may also be a decision to leave a community. Because the armory is the Guard's corporate face, discarding an armory may adversely impact the herald's ability to promote the guard-community relationship without an armory anchor.

The Armory and the Guard's Public Image

At one time, it was taken for granted that the best recruiting opportunities for the National Guard occurred in small agricultural communities. Large metropolitan areas have always hosted multiple units and armories, but recruiting in larger cities has inherent problems. In the late twentieth century, the city worker was suspicious of the Guard as antilabor strike breakers. In the twenty-first century, the low-profile Guard image may be the new hurdle to recruiting in major cities.

The modern highway system appeared to solve the quandary of city enlistment for the Guard. The solution was to recruit from a wider area and let guardsmen drive to their armory site. Unfortunately, commuting removed two characteristics customarily associated with a local Guard company. At one time, Guard unit members were predominately local people who knew the town and its idiosyncrasies. Guardsmen also lived close to the armory, making it possible for them to rapidly assemble in emergencies. Today, many Guard members are commuters; many are unaware of the community fabric where they drill and may be unable to reach the armory quickly in time of need.

Recruiting and commuting are two areas that appear to be intertwined with the trend away from the small-town setting. If there is a vital connection between the small community and the Guard, it remains to be studied. Whether leaving small towns or commuting to the Guard armory are viewed as positive or negative actions, commuting is evidence of an organization adapting to new realities as society changes. Historically, the Guard has demonstrated an ability to adapt as needed. How well the Guard confronts new missions with its inventory of current armories will be judged by the historian.

In 2000, a mid-Missouri newspaper ran a story about a local Guard unit. The reporter's description of the unit's Type 783 armory was revealing, "From the outside, it looks like so many other converted elementary schools built of cold cement block."[3] The reporter could have continued that it looked like a warehouse, a factory, or a jail. Juxtaposing an armory with a warehouse is image confusion that negatively affects the Guard's corporate image.[4] A sign proclaiming a building is in fact an armory is a weak dressing when the whole structure screams warehouse. Modern architecture, like Type 783 armories, has both defenders and detractors. The Type 783 armories serving many Missouri communities have either been accepted in their cityscapes or they have not. But there are aspects of the midcentury modern armory style that should be examined from a Guard perspective, focusing on how Type 783 architecture has served the Guard and how it has or has not earned the Guard respect in the community.

A basic premise of modern architecture is that it represents a universal language that all industrial societies are destined to acquire. Modernists believe simple building shapes are better than ornate structures, which are class-based and outdated, and that society will eventually purge all links to the past and accept the modern style as natural.[5] But is this the best building philosophy for the National Guard? The National Guard grounds its future on the past and thrives in an environment that commemorates the actions of its members. Sanitizing the armory into a multipurpose box effectively removes all vestiges of the Guard's successful corporate culture from the one place where that culture is most visible to the community. Perhaps modern architecture has removed too much and left too little of the past to be representative and beneficial to the Guard. The Type 783 armories were a sign of modernism in their era, but they are also symptomatic of a mentality to build them quickly, cheaply, and uniformly. The armory of the future should not be just a simple and cheap building, but should be a building easily identifiable with the volunteer organization it houses.

One significant aspect of the armory is that it is the sole type of military architecture associated with the National Guard. The armory is indelibly identified with the National Guard and is the Guard's enduring image of itself. Current and former armories are testimonials to the Missouri National Guard's corporate development and a reminder of the Guard's presence in the community.

A number of WPA and Depression-era Missouri National Guard armories are eligible for nomination to the National Register of Historic Places. Many of these armories are no longer attached to the Missouri National Guard, but still serve a function for the local population, and in community memory, are still thought of as armories. Another style becoming eligible for the National Register of Historic Places is the Type 783 armories. They are architecturally not as significant as other styles, but historically they are the embodiment of the Guard during the Cold War period. As a part of that era in American history, the Type 783 armories fulfill one criterion for nomination to the register.

Recognizing former armories as historic buildings is not enough to make them a general benefit to the National Guard. The challenge for supporters of the National Guard—the heralds—is to take buildings identified as former armories and other noteworthy locations in Missouri National Guard history, and raise them from obscurity to the equivalent of venerated "sacred spaces." As a sacred space, the armory is defined as a space or place set apart from the ordinary world because it has great significance for an organization, and recognized by members of that organization as special for various reasons. Often the most sacred spaces in our culture are taken for granted, that is, we know and respect these national sacred spaces without question: Independence Hall, the Washington Mall,

3. Tony Messenger, "Guarded Justice," *Columbia Daily Tribune*, May 7, 2000.

4. Venturi, *Complexity and Contradiction in Architecture*, 93.

5. Brolin, *Failure of Modern Architecture*. 68.

Gettysburg National Battlefield, the White House, the Grand Canyon, and Yosemite National Park. In Missouri, we have the Old St. Louis Courthouse, the Missouri State Capitol, the Pershing Home, Wilson's Creek Battlefield, and Alley Springs. To this list are added Missouri Guard sacred spaces of special significance: Camp Clark, Jefferson Barracks, Fort Belle Fontaine, the St. Louis Soldiers Memorial, and the Liberty Memorial in Kansas City, as well as a number of armories.

Old armories no longer in use and active armories serve different roles for the National Guard. One is set in the present and the other is set in the past, but that does not mean the latter should be forgotten. Someday today's active armory will become the old armory, and just as the active armory serves the Guard today, the former armories serve Guard members as sacred places. The Guard herald must make use of every armory to emphasize to Missourians the past and future role of the Missouri Army National Guard.

Works Cited

Archives

HSTL = Harry S. Truman Library, Independence, Missouri

MMMH = Museum of Missouri Military History, Ike Skelton Training Site, Jefferson City, Missouri

MNGFE = Missouri National Guard Facilities Engineers, Ike Skelton Training Site, Jefferson City, Missouri

MO SHPO = Missouri State Historic Preservation Office, Department of Natural Resources, Jefferson City, Missouri

SHS MO = State Historical Society of Missouri–St. Louis Research Center, St. Louis, Missouri

WHMC = Western Historical Manuscripts Collection, SMS MO

Newspapers and Newsletters

Aurora (MO) Advertiser

Bear Facts (newsletter, MO National Guard)

Boonville (MO) Daily News

Boonville (MO) Weekly Advertiser

Carrollton (MO) Daily Democrat

Carthage (MO) Evening Press

Cass County (MO) Democrat-Missourian

Chillocothe (MO) Constitution-Tribune

Columbia (MO) Daily Tribune

Daily American Republic

Daily Capital News

Daily Sikeston (MO) Standard

Dexter (MO) Statesman

Farmington (MO) News

Fayette (MO) Advertiser

Fulton (MO) Daily Sun-Gazette

Hannibal (MO) Courier-Post

Jefferson County (MO) Journal

Kansas City Star

Kansas City Times

Leader-Journal

Macon (MO) Chronicle-Herald

Macon (MO) Citizen

Malden (MO) Merit

Missouri Intelligencer

Monett (MO) Times

New York Times

Perry County (MO) Sun

Pierce City (MO) Leader-Journal

Sikeston (MO) Herald

St. Louis Globe-Democrat

St. Louis Post-Dispatch

St. Louis Republic

Sullivan's Independent News

Published Sources

"140th Infantry Quarters Remodeled." *Missouri National Guardsman* 3, no. 1 (1953): 3.

Aaltonen, Gaynor. *A History of Architecture: Iconic Buildings Throughout The Ages*. New York: Metro Books, 2008.

Adjutant General. *Annual Report of the Adjutant General, Acting Quartermaster General, Acting Paymaster General, and Acting State Claim Agent of Missouri for the Year Ending December 31, 1869*. Jefferson City: Horace Wilcox, 1870.

———. *Report of the Adjutant General of the State of Missouri to the 32nd General Assembly*. Jefferson City: State Journal, 1883.

———. *Report of the Adjutant General of the State of Missouri for the Years 1897–1898*. Jefferson City: Tribune Printing Co./State Printers and Binders, 1898.

———. *Report of the Adjutant General of the State of Missouri for the Year 1905*. Jefferson City: Hugh Stephens Printing, n.d.

————. *Report of the Adjutant General for the State of Missouri for the Years 1907–1908.* Jefferson City: Hugh Stephens Printing Company, n.d.

————. *Biennial Report of the Adjutant General for the Years 1909–1910.* Jefferson City: Hugh Stephens Printing Company, n.d.

————. *Biennial Report of the Adjutant General of the State of Missouri for the Years 1911–1912.* Jefferson City: Hugh Stephens Printing Company, n.d.

————. *Report of the Adjutant General, State of Missouri, 1915–1916.* Jefferson City: Hugh Stephens Printing, 1917.

Ambrose, Stephen E. *Upton and the Army.* Baton Rouge: Louisiana State University Press, 1964.

Ansell, S. T. "Legal and Historical Aspects of the Militia." *Yale Law Journal* 26, no. 6 (1917): 471–76.

Aurora Centennial Committee. *Aurora Centennial, 1870–1970: Yesterday and Today.* Aurora, MO: MWM Color Press, 1970.

Bek, William G. "The Followers of Duden." *Missouri Historical Review* 16, no. 3 (1922): 343–83.

Bell, Laura. "Castles in America: Their Diffusion into the Northeastern United States During the Romantic Period (1870–1930)." MA thesis, University of Missouri–Columbia, 2008.

Benton, Charlotte, Tim Benton, and Ghislaine Wood, eds. *Art Deco 1910–1939.* Boston: Bulfinch Press, 2003.

Billon, Frederic L. *Annals of St. Louis in Its Early Days under the French and Spanish Dominations.* St. Louis, MO: Frederic L. Billon, 1886.

Blair, Clay. *The Forgotten War, America in Korea 1950–1953.* Annapolis, MD: Naval Institute Press, 1987.

Blake, Peter. *Form Follows Fiasco: Why Modern Architecture Hasn't Worked.* Boston: Little, Brown, 1977.

Boucher, Ronald L. "The Colonial Militia as a Social Institution: Salem, Massachusetts 1765–1775." *Military Affairs* 37 (December 1973): 125–30.

Brolin, Brent C. *The Failure of Modern Architecture.* New York: Van Nostrand Reinhold, 1976.

Callinicos, A. *Against Post-Modernism: A Marxist Critique.* Cambridge: Polity Press, 1989.

Carter, Thomas, and Elizabeth Collins Cromley. *Invitation to Vernacular Architecture: A Guide to the Study of Ordinary Buildings and Landscapes.* Knoxville: University of Tennessee Press, 2005.

Chiei, Chris, and Julie Decker. *The Quonset Hut: Metal Living for a Modern Age.* New York: Princeton Architectural Press, 2005.

Condit, Carl W. *American Building Art.* New York: Oxford University Press, 1961.

Cosmas, Graham A. *An Army for Empire: The United States Army in the Spanish-American War.* Shippensburg, PA: White Mane Publishing, 1994.

Deering, Robert B. "Armory for Columbia, Missouri." In *Let Architectural Concrete Textures Put Life in Your Buildings,* by the Portland Cement Association, 33–35. N.p.: Portland Cement Association, [1941].

Division of Militia Affairs. *Report of the Chief, Division of Militia Affairs in the Office of the Secretary of War Relative to the Organized Militia of the United States, 1910.* Washington DC: US Government Printing Office, 1910.

————. *Report of the Chief, Division of Militia Affairs in the Office of the Secretary of War Relative to the Organized Militia of the United States, 1911.* Washington DC: US Government Printing Office, 1911.

————. *Report of the Chief, Division of Militia Affairs in the Office of the Secretary of War Relative to the Organized Militia of the United States, 1912.* Washington DC: US Government Printing Office, 1912.

Duncan, Alistair. *American Art Deco.* London: Thames and Hudson, 1986.

Ekberg, Carl J. *Colonial Ste. Genevieve: An Adventure on the Mississippi Frontier,* 2nd ed. Tucson, AZ: Patrice Press, 1996.

————. *Francois Vallé and His World: Upper Louisiana before Lewis and Clark.* Columbia: University of Missouri Press, 2002.

Field, George H. *Final Report on the WPA Program, 1935–1943.* Washington DC: Government Printing Office, 1946.

Fogelson, Robert M. *America's Armories: Architecture, Society and Public Order.* Cambridge, MA: Harvard University Press, 1989.

"Four New Armories to Be Constructed." *Missouri National Guardsman* 3, no. 12 (1952): 1–3.

Gebhard, David. *The National Trust Guide to Art Deco in America.* New York: Wiley, 1996.

Gelernter, Mark. *A History of American Architecture, Buildings in Their Cultural and Technological Context.* Hanover, NH: University Press of New England, 1999.

Gowans, Alan. *Styles and Types of North American Architecture: Social Function and Cultural Expression.* New York: Icon

Editions, 1992.

Gray, Gordon. *Reserve Forces for National Security: Report to the Secretary of Defense by the Committee on Civilian Components.* Washington DC: Government Printing Office, 1948.

Hanson, Victor Davis. *Carnage and Culture.* New York: Doubleday, 2001.

Historical Annual: National Guard of the State of Missouri. Jefferson City: Missouri National Guard, 1939.

Holmes, Jack D. L. *Honor and Fidelity: The Louisiana Infantry Regiment and the Louisiana Militia Companies, 1766–1821.* Birmingham, AL: Jack D. L. Holmes, 1965.

House, Jack, ed. *Winston Churchill: His Wit and Wisdom.* London: Hyperion Books, 1965.

Huxtable, Ada Louise. *On Architecture, Collected Reflections in a Century of Change.* New York: Walker, 2008.

Hyde, William, and Howard Conard, eds. *Encyclopedia of the History of St. Louis.* New York: Southern History, 1899.

Jencks, Charles. *What is Post-Modernism?* New York: John Wiley and Sons, 1996.

Johnson, Kathleen Eagen. "Gallant Gothic: Gothic Revival Art at the Philipsburg Manor Gallery." Antiques and the Arts Online; http://antiquesandthearts.com/archive/gothic.htm on line. Excerpted from Johnson, *Gallant Gothic: Selections from the Collection of Historic Hudson Valley.* Exhibit catalog (North Tarrytown, NY: Historic Hudson Valley, 1998).

Keegan, John. *A History of Warfare.* New York: Vintage Books, 1994.

Klein, Marilyn, and David P. Fogle. *Clues to American Architecture.* Washington DC: Starrhill, 1985.

Koch, Robert. "The Medieval Castle Revival: New York Armories." *Society of Architectural Historians* 14 (1955): 23–29.

Kreidberg, Marvin A., and Merton G. Henry. *History of Military Mobilization in the United States Army, 1775–1945.* Department of the Army Pamphlet No. 20-212, 1955.

"Landmarks Letter." *The Arena* 21, no. 4 (1986): 3.

Laver, Harry S. *Citizens More than Soldiers: The Kentucky Militia and Society in the Early Republic.* Lincoln: University of Nebraska Press, 2007.

Laws of the State of Missouri, Passed at the First Regular Session of the Eighty-Third General Assembly, January 9, 1985–June 30, 1985. Jefferson City, MO: Calvin Gunn, 1985.

Laws of the State of Missouri, Passed at the First Session of the Tenth General Assembly, Begun and Held at the City of Jefferson, on Monday, the Nineteenth Day of November, in the Year of Our Lord, One Thousand Eight Hundred and Thirty-Eight. Jefferson City, MO: Calvin Gunn, 1838.

Laws of the State of Missouri, Revised and Digested by Authority of the General Assembly, with an Appendix: Published According to an Act of the General Assembly, passed 21st February, 1825. St. Louis: E. Charless, for the State; Missouri General Assembly, 1825.

Longstreth, Richard. *Main Street: A Guide to American Commercial Architecture.* Washington DC: Preservation Press, 1987.

McCormick, William N. *Design Guide for US Army Reserve Facilities, DG 1110-3-107.* Washington, DC: Corps of Engineers, 1984.

Meyer, Duane G. *The Heritage of Missouri.* St. Louis, MO: River City Publishers, 1982.

Militia Bureau. *Annual Report of the Chief of the Militia Bureau, 1919.* Washington DC: US Government Printing Office, 1920.

———. *Annual Report of the Chief of the Militia Bureau, 1930.* Washington DC: US Government Printing Office, 1930.

Miller, B. E. "Columbia Methodism." In Missouri Methodist Church (Columbia), *The Missouri Methodist Church, Sunday, January 5, 1930.* [Columbia, MO: Herald-Statesman Pub. Co.], 1930.

"National Guard Acquires New Armory." *Missouri National Guardsman* 6, no. 6 (1953): 2.

National Guard Bureau. *Annual Report of the Chief of the National Guard Bureau for the Year Ending 30 June 1936.* Washington DC: US Government Printing Office, 1936.

———. *Annual Report of the Chief of the National Guard Bureau for the Year Ending 30 June 1946.* Washington DC: US Government Printing Office, 1947.

———. *Annual Report of the Chief of the National Guard Bureau for the Year Ending 30 June 1950.* Washington DC: US Government Printing Office, 1951.

———. *Annual Report of the Chief of the National Guard Bureau for the Year Ending 30 June 1951.* Washington DC: US Government Printing Office, 1952.

————. *Annual Report of the Chief of the National Guard Bureau for the Year Ending 30 June 1953.* Washington DC: US Government Printing Office, 1954.

————. *Annual Report of the Chief of the National Guard Bureau for the Year Ending 30 June 1955.* Washington DC: US Government Printing Office, 1956.

————. *Annual Report of the Chief of the National Guard Bureau for the Year Ending 30 June 1956.* Washington DC: US Government Printing Office, 1957.

————. *Annual Report of the Chief of the National Guard Bureau for the Year Ending 30 June 1958.* Washington DC: US Government Printing Office, 1959.

————. *Annual Report of the Chief of the National Guard Bureau for the Year Ending 30 June 1964.* Washington DC: US Government Printing Office, 1965.

————. *Annual Report of the Chief of the National Guard Bureau for the Year Ending 30 June 1984.* Washington DC: US Government Printing Office, 1985.

Nelson, Paula. "Sainte Anne: The Populating of a French Parish in the Illinois Country." MA thesis, Illinois State University, 1993.

"New Armories to Have Recreation Use in Alabama." *American City (Pittsfield, MA)* 70 (1955): 18.

"New-Type Armories are Designed for Expansion." *Architectural Record* 111, no. 3 (June 1952): 14.

Onderdonk, Francis S. *The Ferro-Concrete Style: Reinforced Concrete in Modern Architecture.* New York: Architectural Book Publishing, 1928.

Osgood, Herbert L. *The American Colonies in the Seventeenth Century.* 3 vols. New York: Macmillan, 1904–1907.

Patterson, Tiffany. "Midwest Modern: The Works Progress Administration's Armories of Missouri." Paper presented at 53rd Annual Missouri Conference on History, April 13–15, 2010, Kansas City, Missouri.

Primm, James Neal. *Lion of the Valley: St. Louis, Missouri.* Boulder, CO: Pruett Publishing, 1981.

"Quartermaster Warehouse Centralizes Handling of Supplies, Equipment." *Missouri National Guardsman* 4, no. 5 (1945): 7.

Rafter, DeVere. "The Armory Experience of a Kansas Company." *National Guard Magazine* 8, no. 2 (1911): 105–6.

Reynolds, Lucinda. "History of the Development of a Permanent National Guard Armory in Boonville." MA thesis, Central Methodist College, 1996.

Roth, Leland M. *A Concise History of American Architecture.* New York: Harper and Row, 1980.

Rudofsky, Bernard. *Architecture without Architects: A Short Introduction to Non-Pedigreed Architecture.* Albuquerque: University of New Mexico Press, 1964.

Schart, J. Thomas. *A History of St. Louis City and County.* 2 vols. Philadelphia: L. H. Everts and Co., 1883.

Silber, John. *Architecture of the Absurd: How "Genius" Disfigured a Practical Art.* New York: Quantuck Lane Press, 2007.

Skeen, E. Edward. *Citizen Soldiers in the War of 1812.* Lexington: University Press of Kentucky, 1999.

Stephens, Frank Fletcher. *History of the Missouri Methodist Church of Columbia, Missouri and Its Columbia Predecessors.* Nashville, TN: Parthenon Press, 1965.

Todd, Frederick P. "Our National Guard: An Introduction to Its History." *Military Affairs* 5, no. 2 (1941): 73–86.

Todd, Nancy L. *New York's Historic Armories: An Illustrated History.* New York: SUNY Press. 2006.

US Congress. House. Committee on Armed Services. *Full Committee Hearing on S. 2269, H.R. 8604, S. 2335, H. R. 8594.* Committee Serial No. 192. [Washington, DC: US Government Printing Office], 1950.

US Congress. House. Committee on Armed Services. Brooks Subcommittee. *Subcommittee Hearings on H.R. 8373, to Provide for the Acquisition, Construction, Expansion, Rehabilitation, Conversion, and Joint Utilization of Facilities Necessary for the Administration and Training of Units of the Reserve Components of the Armed Forces of the United States, and for Other Purposes.* [Washington, DC: US Government Printing Office,] 1950.

US Congress. House. Committee on Armed Services. Subcommittee No. 3. *Hearings on H.R. 2824, a Bill to Provide for the Construction, Rehabilitation, Expansion, Conversion, and Joint Utilization of Buildings, Structures, Utilities, and Other Facilities, including the Acquisition of Land, for the Reserve Components of the National Military Establishment of the United States, and for Other Purposes, and H.R. 4750, a Bill to Provide Adequate Facilities for the Training of the Reserve Components of the National Military Establishment and to Promote Full Utilization of All Existing Facilities and All Facilities Hereafter Constructed.* Committee Serial No. 130. [Washington DC: US Government Printing Office,] 1949.

US Congress. House. Conference Committee. *Conference Report to Accompany H.R. 8594, the National Defense Facilities Act of 1950*. 81st Congr., 2nd sess., 1950. H. Doc. 3026. [Washington, DC: US Government Printing Office,] 1950.

US Congress. Senate. *Joint Hearing Before the Subcommittees of the Committees on Military Affairs, 1st sess., on the Construction of National Guard Armories, April 17, 1935*. Washington DC: US Government Printing Office, 1935.

Venturi, Robert. *Complexity and Contradiction in Architecture*. New York: Museum of Modern Art, 1966.

Walker, Bill, Sp/4. "Missouri Guard Acquires New Armory." *Sho-Me Sentinel* 6, no. 2 (Fall 1973): 1–2.

Whiffen, Marcus. *American Architecture since 1780: Guide to the Styles*. Cambridge, MA: MIT Press, 1969.

Wood, Ghislaine. *Essential Art Deco*. Boston: Bulfinch Press, 2003.

Zorinsky, Edward. *Army National Guard: Opportunities to Improve the Condition and Operation of Armories*. Washington DC: Government Printing Office, 1986.

About the Author

After graduating from Westminster College in Fulton, Missouri, Robert P. Wiegers joined the US Army in 1969, and served in Ethiopia, Southeast Asia, and West Germany. Wiegers attended graduate school at Boston University and the University of Missouri-Columbia, where he completed a doctorate in anthropology in 1985. He joined the Missouri Army National Guard in 1986 and completed twenty-five years of combined service in 2004. He took a teaching position at Central Methodist College (now University) in 1989, where he is a professor of history. Wiegers and his wife, Martha, live in Fayette, Missouri. Their two sons, Carey and Trevor, are presently serving with the US Army.

Index

All counties, cities, towns, and villages are in Missouri unless otherwise noted.

OK